# Dollmaking

P9-CLX-902

# Dollmaking

## BY E.J. TAYLOR

### Illustrations by
### ELSA WILLSON

### Photography by
### BELINDA BANKS

## WORKMAN PUBLISHING, NEW YORK

Copyright © 1987 by E.J. Taylor
Photographs © 1987 by Belinda Banks

All rights reserved. No portion of this book
may be reproduced—mechanically,
electronically, or by any other means,
including photocopying—without written
permission of the publisher. Published
simultaneously in Canada by Saunders of
Toronto, Ltd.

Library of Congress Cataloging-in-
Publication Data
Taylor, E.J.      Dollmaking.
1. Dollmaking. I. Title. TT175.T39 1987
745.592′21      87-42745
ISBN 0-89480-311-5 (pbk.)

Art director: Charles Kreloff
Book design: Mark Freiman
Cover and book photographs: Belinda Banks
Book illustrations: Elsa Willson

Antique props used in the photographs
were provided by Tobias and the Angel,
68 White Hart Lane, Barnes, S.W. 13,
London, England.

Workman Publishing Company, Inc.
1 West 39th Street
New York, NY 10018

Manufactured in the United States of
America

First printing November 1987
10  9  8  7  6  5  4  3  2  1

# Dedication

XXXXXXXXXXXXXXXXXXXXXXXXXXXXXXXXXXXXXXXXXXX

This book is dedicated to Biddy

XXXXXXXXXXXXXXXXXXXXXXXXXXXXXXXXXXXXXXXXXXX

# Acknowledgments

XXXXXXXXXXXXXXXXXXXXXXXXXXXXXXXXXXXXXXXXXXX

The contributions to DOLLMAKING of the following people have been enormous and I could not have finished the book without them.

First, a special thanks to Bridget Hayward for all her help and continuous support. Thanks also to Jane Coleman for her back-up work; to Chris Legee, my assistant, for sharing her artistic talent, patience, and brilliant organizational skills; to Amelia Edwards for recommending Chris; to David Delve, for his assistance with the writing of the text; to Yvonne Deutch for editing the first draft; and to Joyce Mason, whose beautiful handlettering ended up on the cutting room floor.

Thanks, too, to Paul Hanson, the designer from Workman, who coincidentally lives in England, for being available during many of the important planning stages of this book.

In New York I would like to thank Charles Hunt and Louise Gault. A very special thanks goes to Ivy Fisher Stone, who loved the book from the first moment it was discussed. Last, but not least, I want to thank Suzanne Rafer at Workman for her brilliant editing and for all her cheerful help to me in the final stages.

# Contents

The Dollmaking Collection, a full-color portfolio of the dolls in this book, appears between pages 64 and 65.

# On Dollmaking

**M**y interest in figure making began when I was seven years old and in elementary school. It was there I saw my first marionette show and could hardly believe the images before my eyes—I was mesmerized.

Soon after I began making puppets. There were always special art projects going on at school and a good supply of papier-mâché on hand. My initial results were a little clumsy since wheat paste and newspaper isn't the easiest medium for achieving fine detail. I did manage, however, to complete some hand puppets, and spent many happy hours acting out stories of my own.

My first dolls were made of materials that were readily available: baling wire I found in our barn (perfect for making armatures, although at the time I didn't know what an armature was), cotton fabric scraps from my mother's quilt box, and white glue from the kitchen drawer.

As my skills developed I progressed to larger projects. One of the first I remember making was a family of pioneers complete with a campfire and covered wagon. Later, I made theaters out of cardboard boxes and designed characters to perform my plays on tabletops (flashlights made excellent spotlights).

I've gone on to create handmade dolls professionally, and am fortunate that my dolls have been displayed in the windows of Tiffany's, Henri Bendel's, and Saks Fifth Avenue in New York City, used in Broadway shows, and chosen by the American Ballet Theater for their production of <u>The Nutcracker.</u>

But you don't have to have professional aspirations to create beautiful dolls. Anyone who understands some of the basic techniques can succeed. A cloth doll is an easy way to start. Fabric is inexpensive, and if there are problems it's easy to start over. I do think, though, that it is sometimes nice to let the mistakes show—they often give character to the doll.

Know that your effort will always show through in the finished piece, especially if you take care with details. I do everything including the stitching by hand, and suggest that all dollmakers do the same. In a world where everything is made by machines, the satisfaction of making something entirely by hand is uniquely rewarding. Remember, every handmade doll has a very special endearing quality—it is the only one of its kind.

# The Dolls

# A Simple Rag Doll

There are three versions of this doll —all easy and fun to make. The basic shape is a free-form silhouette. I don't dress this doll up, and I don't worry if the measurements are not exact, or if one side is longer than the other. So, feel free about it. Use small stitches and enjoy making every detail by hand. To add a look of age and character to the doll, I stain my unbleached muslin with tea or coffee.

## You Will Need

2 sheets heavy white typing paper
Soft pencil
Tape measure
Scissors
1 yard unbleached muslin
Pins
Needles
Thread (an assortment)
Kapok stuffing
Knitting needle
Set of watercolors with a paint brush
Bowl of clean water
Button thread

# Drawing and Cutting

x x x x x x x x x x x x x x x x x x x x x x x x x x x x x x x x x x x x x x x x

**1** Lay a sheet of typing paper on a flat surface. With the soft pencil, drawing freehand, copy 1 of the basic shapes from Fig.1. Shapes A and B are about 9 inches long, and shape C is about 6 inches long.

Take care to make the head a reasonable size. The width of the head should be at least 2 inches, the length of the head should be at least 2½ inches, and the width of the neck should be at least 1½ inches (Fig. 2).

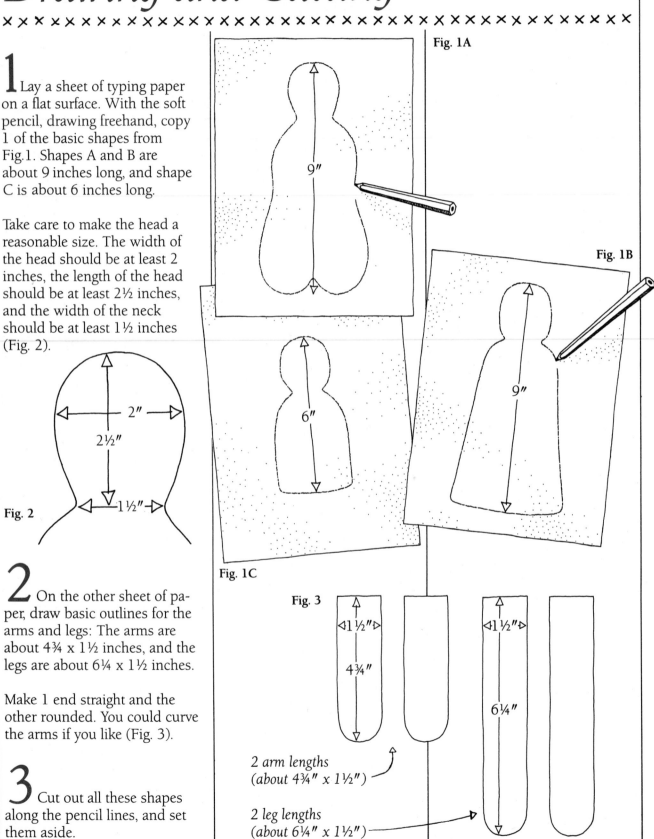

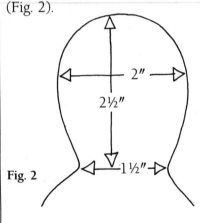

Fig. 1A

Fig. 1B

Fig. 1C

Fig. 2

Fig. 3

**2** On the other sheet of paper, draw basic outlines for the arms and legs: The arms are about 4¾ x 1½ inches, and the legs are about 6¼ x 1½ inches.

Make 1 end straight and the other rounded. You could curve the arms if you like (Fig. 3).

**3** Cut out all these shapes along the pencil lines, and set them aside.

2 arm lengths
(about 4¾" x 1½")

2 leg lengths
(about 6¼" x 1½")

**4** Take the unbleached muslin, and cut out a piece 24 x 12 inches. Lay this flat.

**5** Fold the muslin in half, creating 2 layers about 12 inches square. Pin this along the edges (Fig. 4).

**Fig. 4**

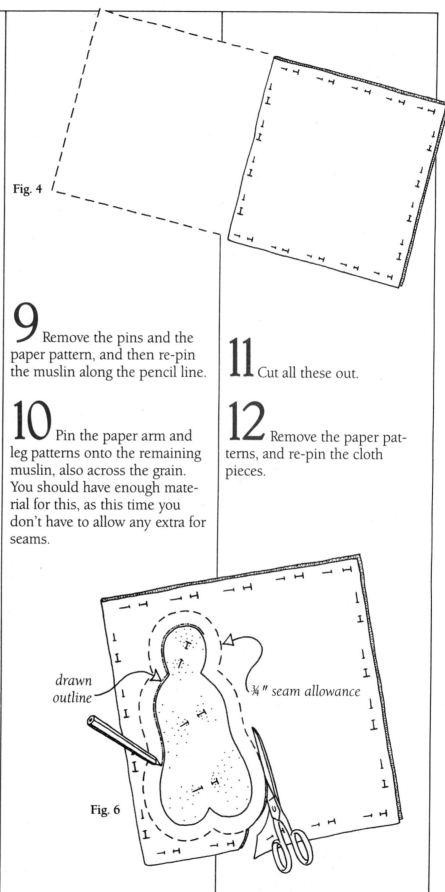

**6** Take the paper body shape and pin it to the muslin, leaving room for ¾-inch seams all the way around. Make sure that the pattern lies across the grain of the muslin (Fig. 5).

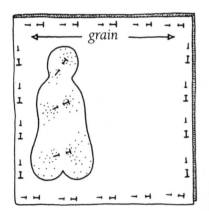

grain

**Fig. 5**

**7** With your pencil, lightly trace the outline onto the muslin.

**8** Take the scissors, and adding ¾ inch all around for seams, cut out the silhouette from the muslin (Fig. 6).

**9** Remove the pins and the paper pattern, and then re-pin the muslin along the pencil line.

**10** Pin the paper arm and leg patterns onto the remaining muslin, also across the grain. You should have enough material for this, as this time you don't have to allow any extra for seams.

**11** Cut all these out.

**12** Remove the paper patterns, and re-pin the cloth pieces.

drawn outline

¾ " seam allowance

**Fig. 6**

# Stitching and Stuffing

×××××××××××××××××××××××××××××××××××××××××××××××××

**13** Thread a needle with regular thread, and taking the muslin body shape, sew the layers together all along the pencil line with a running stitch, leaving a 1½-inch gap at 1 shoulder (Fig. 7).

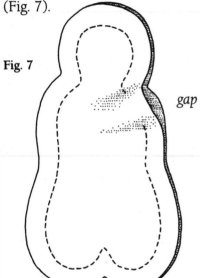

**Fig. 7**

*gap*

**14** Take each arm and leg shape, and allowing for a small ¼-inch seam, sew those layers together with a running stitch, leaving the straight end open (Fig. 8).

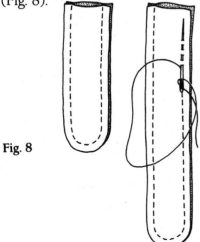

**Fig. 8**

**15** Take your scissors and snip the seam allowance on the curves in the body and around the bottom of the arm and leg shapes (Figs. 9A and 9B).

**Fig. 9A**

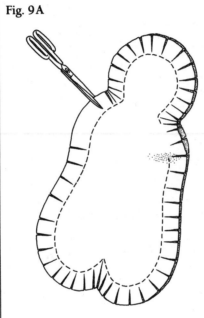

**Fig. 9B**

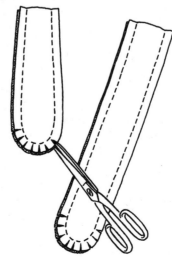

**16** Turn all the pieces right side out.

**17** Take some of the Kapok stuffing and push it through the gap left in the body shape, using a long implement such as a knitting needle or a pencil. Push well down into the corners first, and continue until you have filled it really tight. When you reach the gap, overfill with stuffing. Then, folding in the open seams, close with a pin parallel to the stitched seam (Fig. 10).

**Fig. 10**

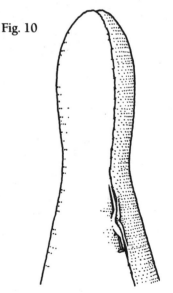

**18** Take your needle and thread, and secure the pinned gap with an overcast stitch.

**19** I find it's a good idea at this stage to double-stitch the neck curves to reinforce them.

**20** Using a different-colored thread (I like a pastel shade), overcast the seams around the entire body shape (Fig. 11). Set this aside.

Fig. 11

**21** Now take each limb shape in turn and pack it with the stuffing—but not as tightly as the body, and only up to 1 inch from the open end.

**22** Fold in ½ inch of the fabric at each open end. Press tightly around the edge to create a crease. The stuffing should now be ½ inch from this crease (Fig. 12). This will allow movement of the doll's arms and legs.

Fig. 12

**23** Pin the open end of each limb to its respective place on the main body shape (Fig. 13).

Fig. 13

**24** Stitch the arms and legs to the body with regular thread. Unpin.

**25** Using the different-colored thread, overcast the arm and leg seams (but not the seams that join the arms and legs to the torso).

**26** Now your basic doll shape is ready.

I often stitch a false seam down the center of the body, using a pastel thread. This is optional, but I feel it enhances the hand-made quality.

Another addition I like to make sometimes are small darns (Fig. 14).

Fig. 14

*darn*

*darn*

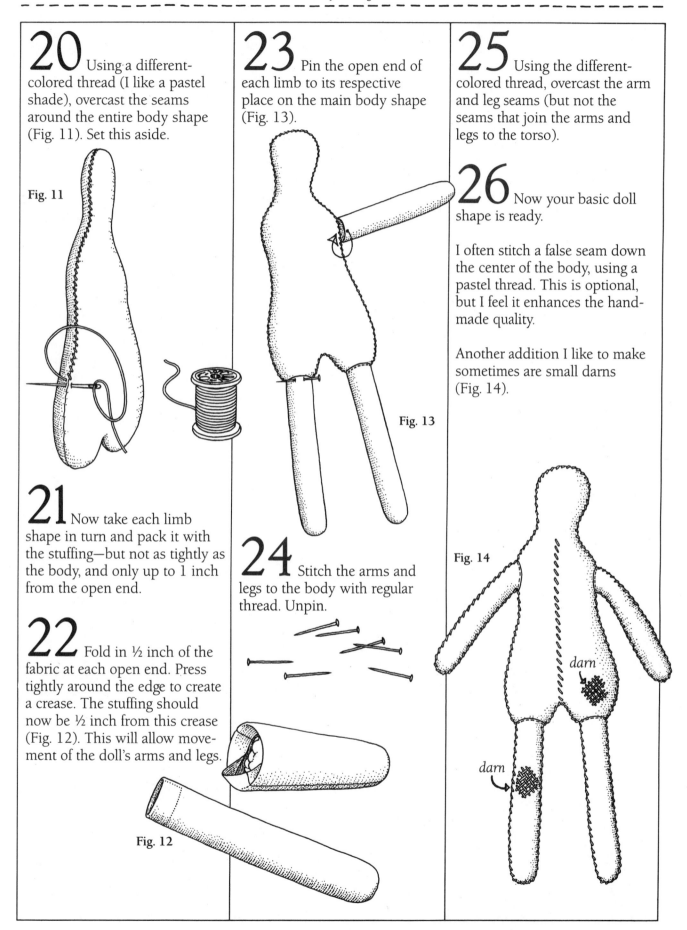

# 27 The Eyes: Take a dark thread (blue, brown, or purple) and embroider 2 solid eyes (Fig. 15).

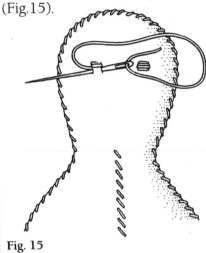

**Fig. 15**

# 28 The Nose: Cut a small triangular shape out of muslin. Fold as shown (Fig. 16 A–16D).

**Fig. 16A**

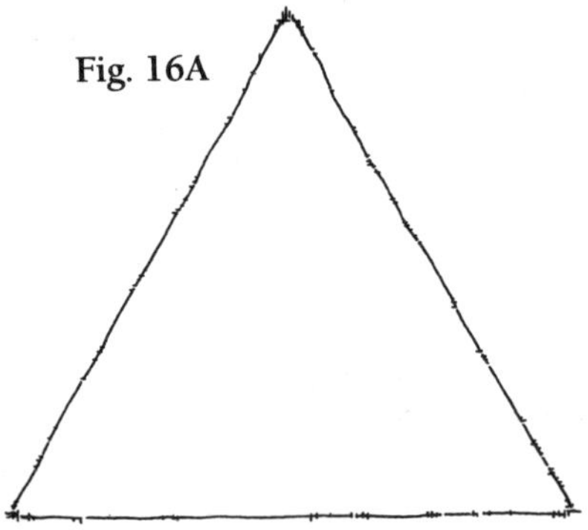

**Fig. 16B**

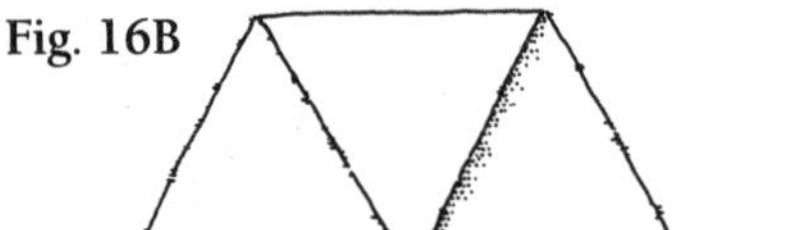

**Fig. 16C**

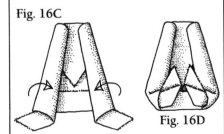

**Fig. 16D**

Bunch it tightly into a nose shape, and pin it to the face (Fig. 17). Sew the nose to the face, using invisible stitches.

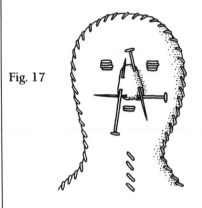

**Fig. 17**

# 29 The Mouth: Use a short stitch to make a mouth line with orange or red thread (Fig. 17).

# 30 Color: This helps to give the face a little more dimension. Take your paintbrush and wet the entire face with clean water. (This helps the colors blend when they are applied.) Mix a pale red wash, and without making the brush too wet each time, dab on a spot for each cheek (Fig. 18).

Let this dry, then add another layer to darken it. Repeat this until you have the tone you like, remembering that it is simple to make a watercolor darker, but it's impossible to lighten it.

Next make a pale blue wash, and paint around the eyes. Dab it around the nose seam as well.

A light brown wash painted on all the overcast seams will add interest.

# 31 The Hair: Thread a medium-size needle with double button thread—choose a complementary color to your muslin (I usually use a beige). Make it nice and long to save constant re-threading.

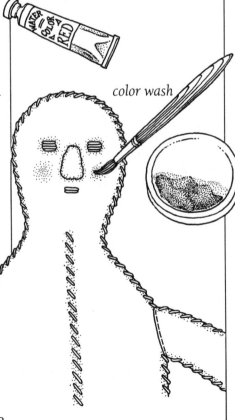

*color wash*

**Fig. 18**

**32** Make a small stitch on the back of the head at the lowest point you want the hair to be. Then pull the thread through until the tail end is the length you desire (Fig. 19A).

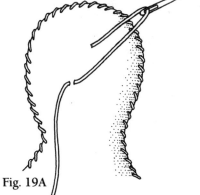

**Fig. 19A**

Make 2 small stitches over this one to secure it (Fig. 19B).

**Fig. 19B**

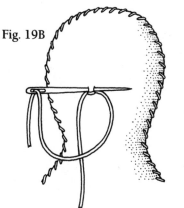

Cut the thread off at the required length (Fig. 19C).

**Fig. 19C**

**33** Continue with this until you have sufficient hair. But I do warn you that this can be a long job, and requires a lot of patience. As you can see from the illustration of the 3 sample dolls, you can vary the length of hair as you wish, and also make up your own hairstyles—for example, a ponytail, bun, or braid.

**34** Your rag doll is now complete, but as a final touch I often sew on a pocket—with a tiny button on it for fun (Fig. 20).

**Fig. 20**

# A Dressed Rag Doll

The Dressed Rag Doll is an extension of the Simple Rag Doll. It is a little more refined since it has a pattern—although the pattern is not at all a rigid one. You can easily adapt this doll to suit your own taste. Choose unusual buttons for the eyes, mix different-colored yarns for the hair, and vary the clothing. The only requirements for rag dolls are that they should be floppy and fun.

## You Will Need

Scissors
Brown wrapping paper
Pencil and ruler
1¼ yards unbleached muslin
Pins
Yellow or blue carbon tracing paper
Tailor's tracing wheel
Tape measure (use as needed)
Needles
Thread
Kapok stuffing
Long-handled wooden spoon
Buttons for face and dress
Embroidery thread (red and cream)
Bowl of clean water
1 tablespoon instant coffee
¼ cup boiling water
Set of watercolors with a paintbrush
Piece of cardboard, 3 x 10 inches
Yarn for hair
1 yard cotton print dress fabric
Steam iron
Ribbon
Baby socks and shoes

# Making a Pattern

×××××××××××××××××××××××××××××××××××××××××××××××

I use brown wrapping paper to make patterns, as it is easy to get where I live. Large grocery bags, split open and pressed flat, will work equally well.

**1** Cut out a piece of brown wrapping paper to measure at least 24 x 15 inches. With your pencil and ruler, draw a grid of 1-inch squares on the paper, as shown in Fig. 1. Letter the squares across, and number those down.

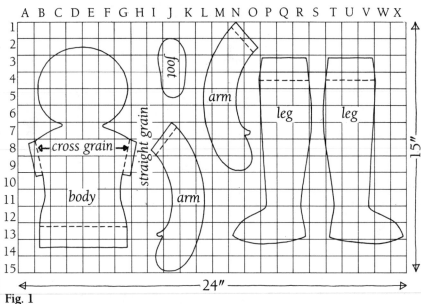

Fig. 1

**2** Following Fig. 1, draw the pattern shapes on the grid, so that you finish up with 1 body shape, 2 arms, 2 legs, and 1 foot.

**3** Cut out these paper patterns.

**4** Lay the unbleached muslin on a flat surface, then fold it in half lengthways, and smoothly and evenly pin all around the edges.

**5** Lay the paper pattern pieces on the muslin, allowing at least 1 inch space between them. Pin them on. Make sure that you follow Fig. 1 exactly to match the grain of the fabric. Cut the pattern pieces out of the muslin, adding a ¼-inch seam allowance around each pattern.

**6** Lay a piece of carbon tracing paper beneath each cutout piece, carbon side facing the muslin, and trace around the paper pattern with the tracing wheel. Include all the pattern markings (Fig. 2).

**7** Unpin and remove the paper patterns, then re-pin the muslin pieces. Turn them over, place them on the carbon paper, and repeat the tracing process, this time following the carbon lines on the muslin. Check to make sure that you have included all the lines of the pattern on both sides.

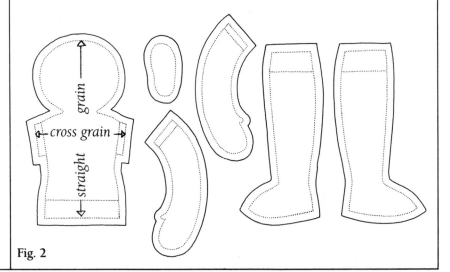

Fig. 2

# Sewing the Body Together

**8** Take the body shape, and following the letter guide in Fig. 3, pin A–D, E–J, and K–N along the traced lines. Then sew the layers together with a small running stitch. This leaves both armholes and the base of the body open (Fig. 3).

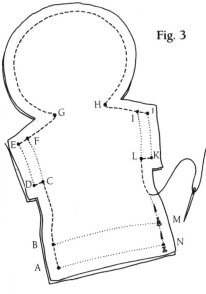

**Fig. 3**

**9** Take your scissors and snip the seam allowance at 1-inch intervals around the head and neck. At points G and H, snip as close as you can to the seam (Fig. 4).

**Fig. 4**

**10** Turn the whole shape right side out, and smooth it on a flat surface. Use an overcast stitch to reinforce the neck at points G and H (Fig. 5).

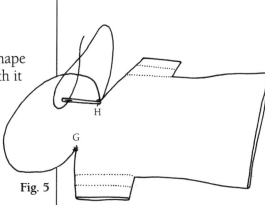

**Fig. 5**

**11** Pin the armholes closed (F–C and I–L). Sew these lines up with a running stitch (Fig. 6).

**Fig. 6**

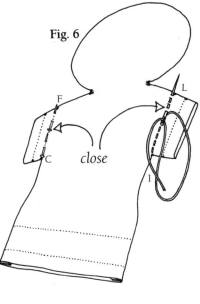

*close*

**12** Now fill the body shape with stuffing through the bottom opening (A–N). Push it down well—a long-handled wooden spoon is useful—and pack it tight and firm. Stop filling when you reach the line B–M on the figure (Fig. 7).

*Kapok*

**Fig. 7**

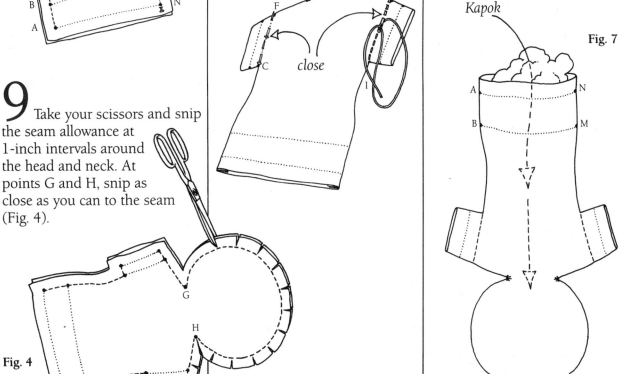

# 13
Stitch the base closed using small overcast stitches, following the method shown in Figs. 8A–8E. It's a bit like neatly gift wrapping a box.

**Fig. 8A**

*Fold ½" all around.*

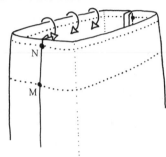

**Fig. 8B**

*Fold one side down and then the other.*

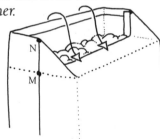

**Fig. 8C**

*Pin and overcast the seam.*

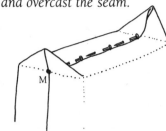

**Fig. 8D**

*Fold ends down,      pin,*

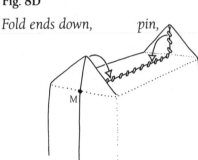

**Fig. 8E**

*then overcast.*

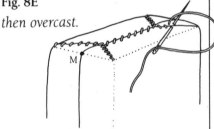

# 14
Fold in a ¼-inch seam allowance at the end of each arm along lines E–D and J–K, and pin them closed. Then stitch them together with an overcast stitch (Fig. 9A-9B).

**Fig. 9A**

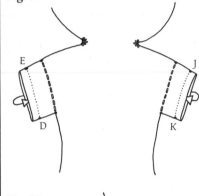

**Fig. 9B**

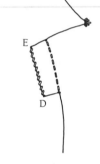

# Filling in the Face

# 15
Take 3 buttons—they can be any kind you like, but the 2 for the eyes should be the same, about 1 inch in diameter. I find 4-holed buttons more expressive for the eyes, and use a ½-inch 2-holed button for the nose. Lay these on the face in a position that you like. When you are happy with the result, mark the positions with a pencil.

# 16
Take a 4-inch piece of red embroidery thread, and arrange it on the face in any mouth shape that you like. Follow this line with a light pencil mark (Fig. 10).

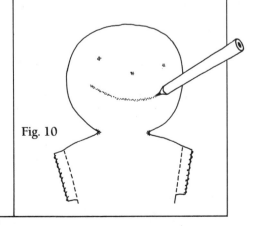

**Fig. 10**

**17** Attach the buttons about ¼ inch away from the head with a firm button stitch (Fig. 11).

**18** Embroider the mouth line in red.

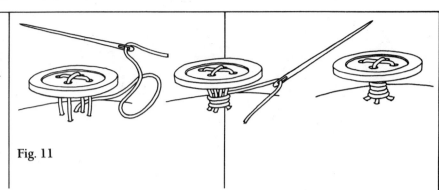

**Fig. 11**

# Painting the Face

Remember, when painting in watercolor, always start with a light wash and gradually add more color.

**19** Wet the muslin face all over with clean water.

Make a light coffee wash by mixing 1 tablespoon instant coffee with ¼ cup boiling water. Dip a dry paintbrush into the wash and dab it along the seams, and at random over the

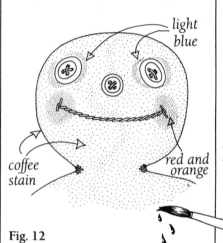

light blue

coffee stain

red and orange

**Fig. 12**

face. Doing this in an irregular manner helps give the face depth and tone (Fig. 12).

**20** Dab on red and orange wash for the cheeks and a light blue wash around the eyes.

# Sewing on the Hair

**21** Mark a point at the center top of the doll's head, and also at the center of the back of the neck. Using a ruler, pencil in a line joining these two points (Fig. 13A).

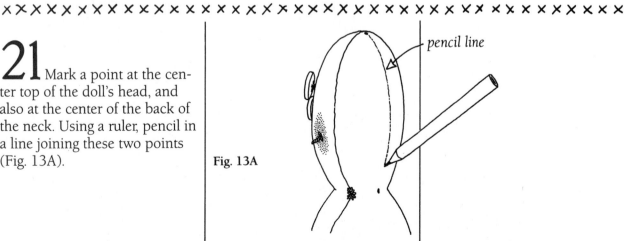

pencil line

**Fig. 13A**

**22** Mark off every ½ inch down this line (Fig. 13B). Then mark straight lines through these points across the back of the head (Fig. 13C).

Fig. 13B

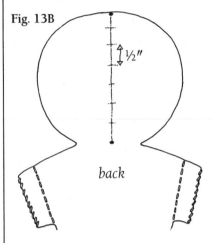

back

Fig. 13C

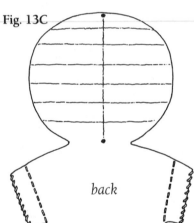

back

**23** Take a piece of cardboard measuring 3 inches by whatever length you want the hair to be—in this case, 10 inches. Wrap as much yarn around this as you can, and then cut through it all at 1 end. Repeat if you need more (Fig. 14).

Fig. 14

cardboard

**24** Take 2 strands of yarn, fold them in half, and stitch them to the back of the head as illustrated (Figs. 15A–15C): Start on the lowest ruled line, place them ¼ inch apart, and anchor each point with 4 tiny overcast stitches. Continue along the lines until they are all filled in.

Fig. 15A

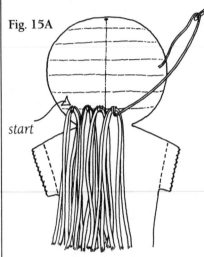

start

Fig. 15B

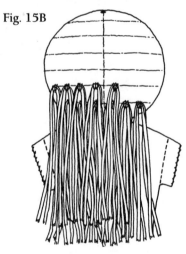

Fig. 15C

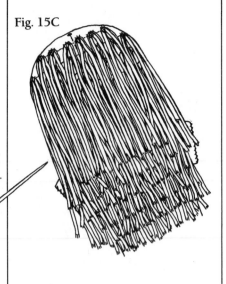

**25** Take the seam around the head as the hairline and stitch the final row of yarn lengths flush together along this line. Trim off any uneven lengths (Fig. 16).

Fig. 16

# Attaching the Arms

× × × × × × × × × × × × × × × × × × × × × × × × × × × × × × × × × × × × × × × × × × ×

**26** Take 1 set of arm pieces and with your pencil lightly mark A on one side, B on the other. Do the same with the other arm set. Remove the pins, and pair up the A pieces and the B pieces. You should have the carbon lines Q–R and S–T already marked on your pattern pieces, as shown in Fig. 17.

**Fig. 17**

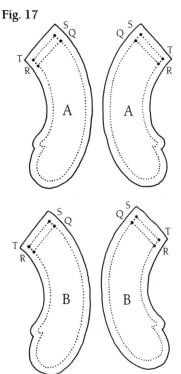

**27** Pin the A pieces together (marked side out), matching all the markings carefully. Do the same with the B pieces. Sew them together with a small running stitch along the traced lines. Leave the armholes open (Fig. 17).

**28** Snip the seam allowance at 1-inch intervals all the way around. Snip more closely around the curve and very closely around the thumb joint (Fig. 18).

**Fig. 18**

*snip allowance*

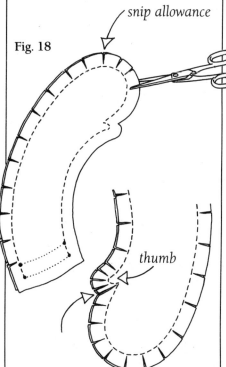

*thumb*

**29** Turn the arms right side out, and reinforce the thumb joint area with overcast stitching (Fig. 19).

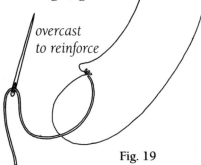

*overcast to reinforce*

**Fig. 19**

**30** Stuff each arm with Kapok up to the line R–Q. Pin along the line, then sew it closed with a running stitch (Fig. 20).

*turn in*

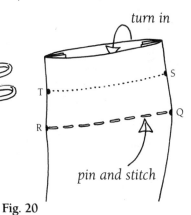

*pin and stitch*

**Fig. 20**

**31** Turn in the ¼-inch seam allowance along line T–S. Pin and close it off with overcast stitching (Fig. 21).

**Fig. 21**

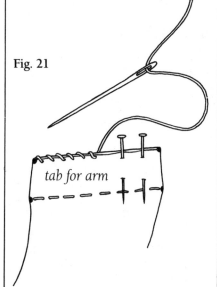

*tab for arm*

**32** To attach the arms to the shoulders, lay the doll's body, face up, on a table. Place arm A with the thumb toward the body on the right side. Pin the arm flap over the body flap. Repeat this procedure for the other arm (Fig. 22A). Then attach the arms with a firm overcast stitch (Fig. 22B–22C).

**Fig. 22A**

stitch

**Fig. 22B**

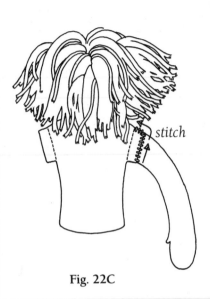

stitch

**Fig. 22C**

# Getting the Legs Straight

**33** Mark the muslin leg pieces A and B as you did for the arms in Step 26. Unpin and match up the A pieces and the B pieces (Fig. 23).

**34** You should have all the carbon pattern markings traced on your muslin pattern pieces, as shown in Fig. 23.

**35** Pin the side seams of each leg together (R–T and Q–U), and sew them up with small running stitches along the traced line.

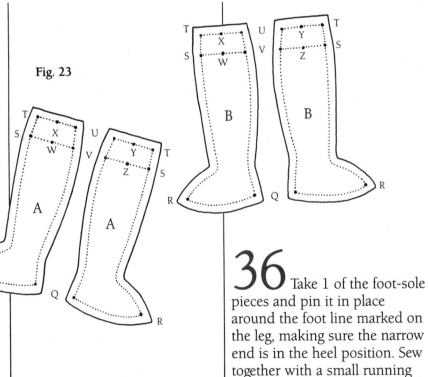

**Fig. 23**

**36** Take 1 of the foot-sole pieces and pin it in place around the foot line marked on the leg, making sure the narrow end is in the heel position. Sew together with a small running

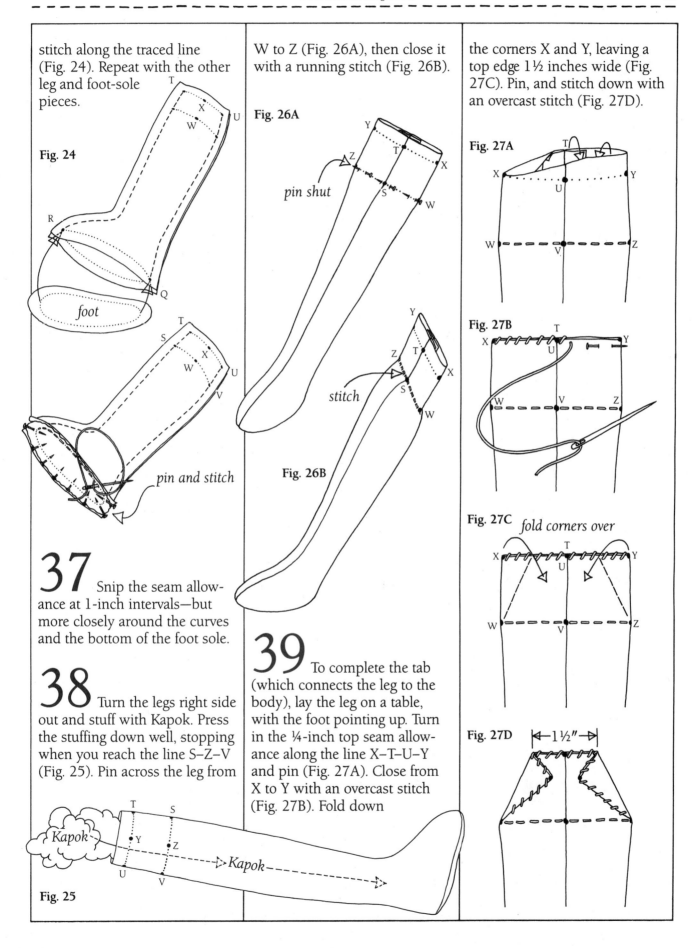

stitch along the traced line (Fig. 24). Repeat with the other leg and foot-sole pieces.

**Fig. 24**

*foot*

*pin and stitch*

**37** Snip the seam allowance at 1-inch intervals—but more closely around the curves and the bottom of the foot sole.

**38** Turn the legs right side out and stuff with Kapok. Press the stuffing down well, stopping when you reach the line S–Z–V (Fig. 25). Pin across the leg from

*Kapok*

*Kapok*

**Fig. 25**

W to Z (Fig. 26A), then close it with a running stitch (Fig. 26B).

**Fig. 26A**

*pin shut*

*stitch*

**Fig. 26B**

**39** To complete the tab (which connects the leg to the body), lay the leg on a table, with the foot pointing up. Turn in the ¼-inch top seam allowance along the line X–T–U–Y and pin (Fig. 27A). Close from X to Y with an overcast stitch (Fig. 27B). Fold down

the corners X and Y, leaving a top edge 1½ inches wide (Fig. 27C). Pin, and stitch down with an overcast stitch (Fig. 27D).

**Fig. 27A**

**Fig. 27B**

**Fig. 27C** *fold corners over*

**Fig. 27D** 1½"

**40** Turn the doll upside down and pin the legs to the bottom seam of the body (Fig. 28A). Turn the right way to check that they both hang correctly—and adjust if necessary. Attach them to the body with an overcast stitch (Fig. 28B).

**Fig. 28A**

**Fig. 28B**

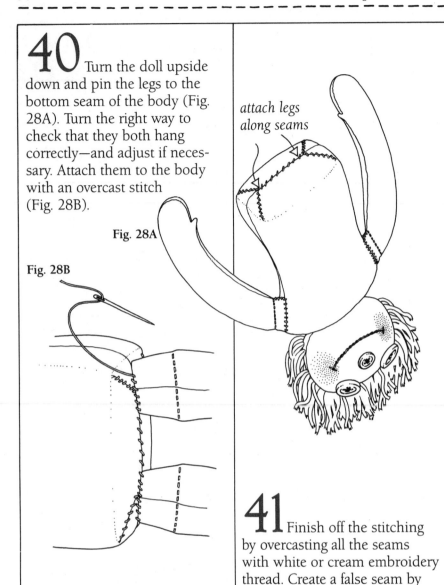

*attach legs along seams*

**41** Finish off the stitching by overcasting all the seams with white or cream embroidery thread. Create a false seam by

running a line of overcast stitching down the front of the face (Fig. 29).

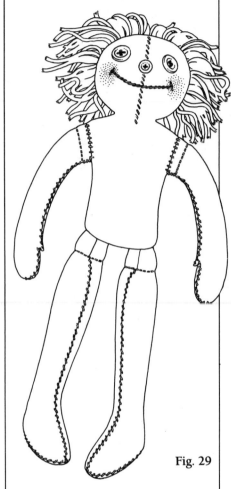

**Fig. 29**

# Dressing the Doll

It is possible to dress this doll in old baby clothes that you happen to have, or that you find when rummaging through thrift shops. Personally, I like to make the dress myself, and then add some interesting accessories such as socks, shoes, and a sweater.

**42** Using the same grid method as for the doll pattern, transfer the dress pattern onto brown wrapping paper 30 x 15 inches. You will have 5 pattern pieces—skirt, front and back bodice, sleeve, and neck facing. Cut these out (Fig. 30).

**43** Lay the front bodice and neck-facing patterns on a single layer of your dress fabric. Pin them on, allowing for ½-inch seams all around.

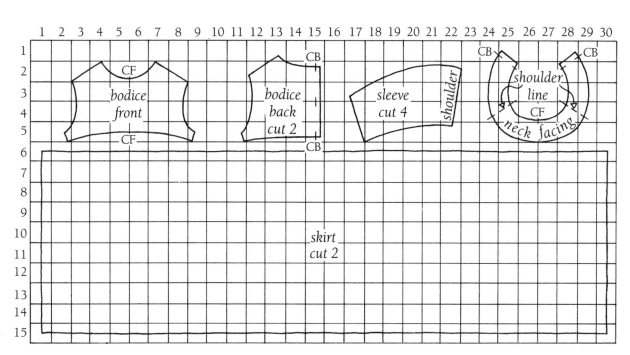

**Fig. 30**

Lay the skirt, back bodice, and sleeve patterns on an evenly folded piece of the fabric. Pin and cut these out, allowing ½ inch all around for seams. Cut the sleeve pattern out twice, to make 4 sleeve pieces in all.

**44** Take the 3 bodice pieces—1 front and 2 back—and pin these together, right sides facing in, at the shoulder and side seams, leaving the back seam open. Stitch the seams together with a running stitch, allowing a ½-inch seam allowance (Fig. 31).

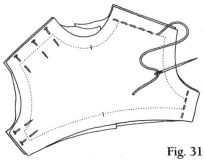

**Fig. 31**

**45** Stitch the skirt pieces together along one of the short sides, allowing a ½-inch seam allowance, and press open the seam.

**46** Keeping the skirt piece wrong side out, make a loose running stitch ¼ inch in from the top, and gather loosely (Fig. 32). Pin the center skirt seam to the center of the front of the bodice. Arrange the skirt to fit by pulling the gathering thread evenly. The open ends of the skirt meet at the center back of the bodice. Still keeping the wrong side out, pin the skirt to the bodice, and stitch together using small running stitches, with a ½-inch seam allowance.

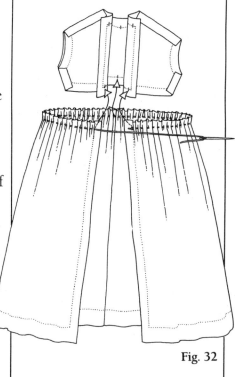

**Fig. 32**

**47** Pin together the back seam of the skirt from the bottom to 2½ inches below the bodice line (Fig. 33). Stitch it up with running stitches.

**Fig. 33**

**48** Press all the seams flat, and turn the dress right side out.

**49** Take the neck-facing piece and pin it around the bodice neckline, right sides facing, allowing ½ inch for seams. Match the center back (CB) and center front (CF) marks (Fig. 34). Stitch with running stitches.

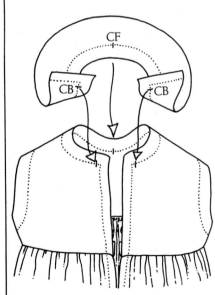

CF

CB

CB

**Fig. 34**

**50** Trim the collar seam to ¼ inch and snip the seam at ½-inch intervals, snipping more at the shoulder area of the curve (Fig. 35).

*trim and snip*

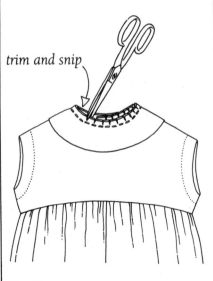

**Fig. 35**

**51** Turn the neck facing to the inside of the bodice, and press it flat (Fig 36A).

**52** Turn in the back seam allowance of the bodice and stitch. Turn in the end of the neck facing and tack it down. Tack the neck facings to the shoulder seams (Fig. 36B).

**Fig. 36A**

*turn in*

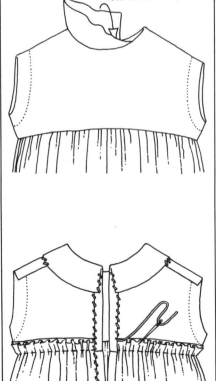

**Fig. 36B**

**53** Pin together each pair of sleeve pieces, right sides facing, then stitch the upper and lower seams together with running stitches, allowing ½-inch seams (Fig. 37). Turn the dress wrong side out and fit, then pin the sleeves into each armhole, matching the upper seams to the shoulder seams. Finally, stitch them into place with running stitches.

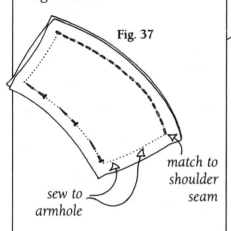

**Fig. 37**

sew to armhole

match to shoulder seam

**54** Turn the dress right side out and fit it onto your doll. Take up the skirt and sleeve hems to the lengths you want.

**55** To fix the back openings, use 2 or 3 small buttons, and make eyeloops with embroidery thread (Fig. 38).

**Fig. 38**

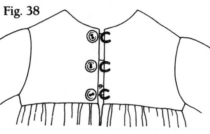

**56** Add ribbons for bows in the hair, and any other accessories or trim that you wish. You now have your very own dressed-up rag doll.

# A Paper Doll

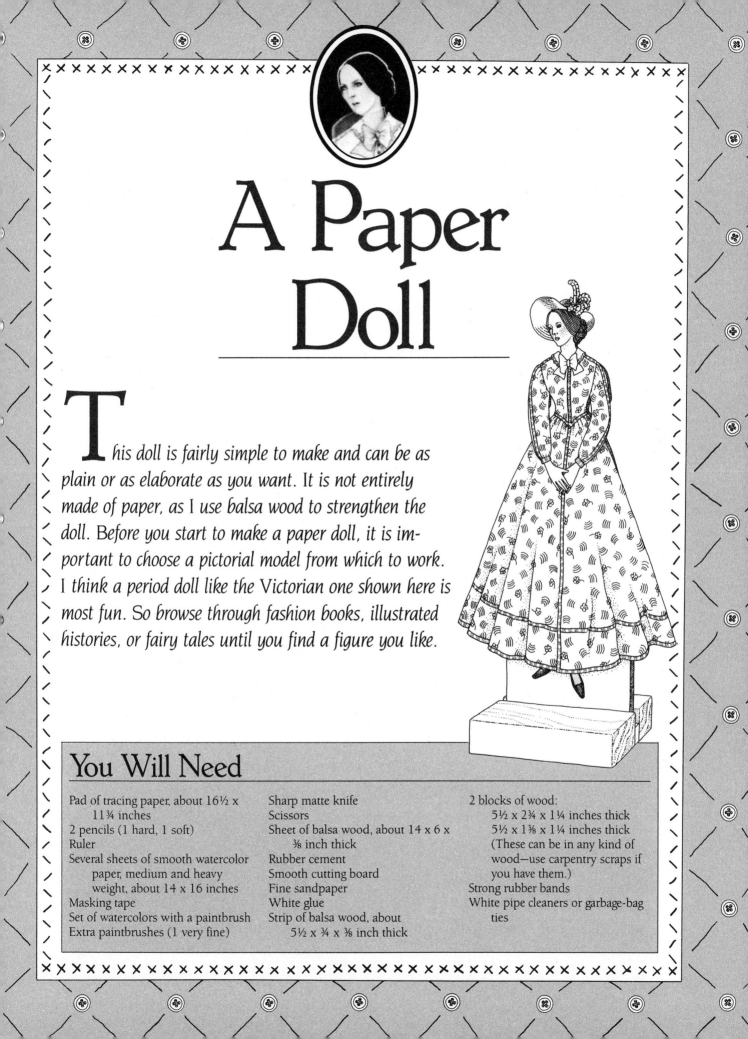

**T**his doll is fairly simple to make and can be as plain or as elaborate as you want. It is not entirely made of paper, as I use balsa wood to strengthen the doll. Before you start to make a paper doll, it is important to choose a pictorial model from which to work. I think a period doll like the Victorian one shown here is most fun. So browse through fashion books, illustrated histories, or fairy tales until you find a figure you like.

## You Will Need

Pad of tracing paper, about 16½ x 11¾ inches
2 pencils (1 hard, 1 soft)
Ruler
Several sheets of smooth watercolor paper, medium and heavy weight, about 14 x 16 inches
Masking tape
Set of watercolors with a paintbrush
Extra paintbrushes (1 very fine)

Sharp matte knife
Scissors
Sheet of balsa wood, about 14 x 6 x ⅜ inch thick
Rubber cement
Smooth cutting board
Fine sandpaper
White glue
Strip of balsa wood, about 5½ x ¾ x ⅜ inch thick

2 blocks of wood:
   5½ x 2¾ x 1¼ inches thick
   5½ x 1⅜ x 1¼ inches thick
   (These can be in any kind of wood—use carpentry scraps if you have them.)
Strong rubber bands
White pipe cleaners or garbage-bag ties

# Making a Pattern

× × × × × × × × × × × × × × × × × × × × × × × × × × × × × × × × × × × × × × × × ×

**1** Take a piece of tracing paper and lay it on a flat, firm surface. Using a hard pencil and a ruler, mark off intervals of 1½ inches, starting at ½ inch down. Draw straight lines through these points across the paper—you should have 9 (Fig. 1).

**Fig. 1**

**Fig. 2**

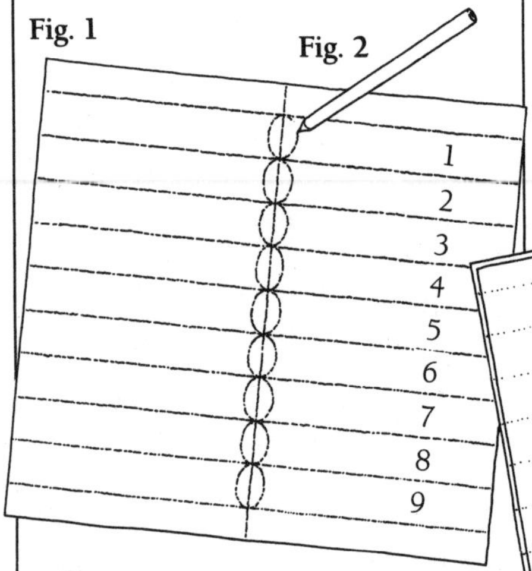

1
2
3
4
5
6
7
8
9

**2** Measure halfway across your paper and draw a faint vertical line. Around this line, draw oval head shapes in all the 1½-inch areas. This doll figure is 9 heads high (Fig. 2).

**3** Draw a human figure around the ovals, as shown—shoulders just above the bottom of the second oval and knees in line with the center of the seventh oval (Fig. 3).

**Fig. 3**

**4** Using this shape as a guide, lay another piece of tracing paper over it, and draw the stance for your doll's figure—either three-quarter view or full face is best.

Draw a hairstyle that leaves the neck and shoulders free. The hands and arms can be drawn extended or crossed in front of the torso (Fig. 4).

**Fig. 4**

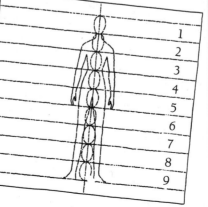

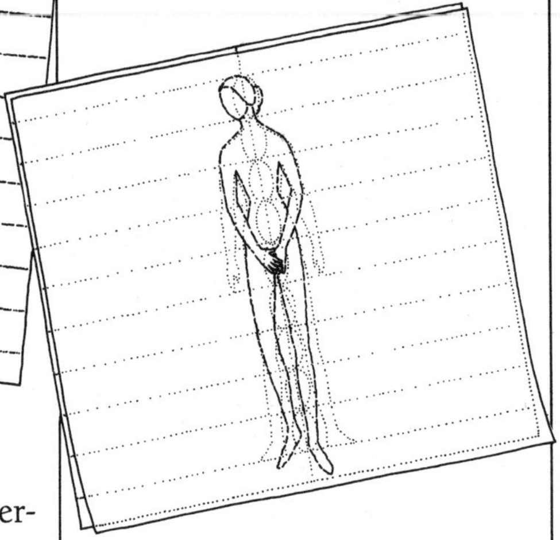

1
2
3
4
5
6
7
8
9

**5** Trace the figure onto a third piece of tracing paper, and sketch over it until you have a detailed drawing that pleases you. This includes facial features, underwear, stockings, shoes, etc. The sample doll is wearing a plain petticoat (Fig. 5).

**Fig. 5**

**6** When it is complete, turn your final piece of tracing paper over. Shade the reverse side thoroughly with a soft pencil (Fig. 6).

**Fig. 6**

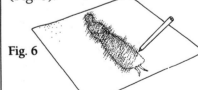

**7** Take a sheet of medium-weight watercolor paper, preferably a bit larger than your tracing paper, and lay it on a flat surface. With masking tape, secure the top corners of the tracing paper to the top of the watercolor paper, shaded side facing the watercolor paper.

**8** Trace over the detailed drawing with the hard pencil. Lift the tracing paper regularly to check that you haven't left out an eye, a pleat, a hand (Fig. 7).

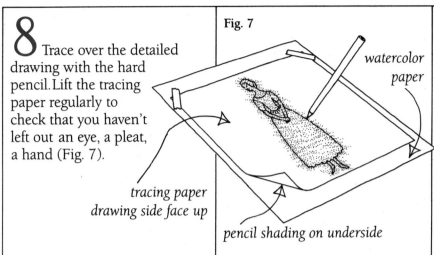

Fig. 7

*watercolor paper*

*tracing paper drawing side face up*

*pencil shading on underside*

**9** Take away the tracing paper, and emphasize the line on the watercolor paper with a hard pencil.

**10** Repeat this transfer sequence onto another watercolor sheet, so that you have 2 drawn figures on separate sheets. Set 1 aside.

× × × × × × × × × × × × × × × × × × × × × × × × × × × × × × × × × × × × × × × × ×

# Painting the Figure

× × × × × × × × × × × × × × × × × × × × × × × × × × × × × × × × × × × × × × × × ×

If you are in any doubt about working with watercolor paints, you should be able to find a basic instruction book in your local library. The most important thing to remember when using watercolors is that you should always begin with a light wash and gradually build to a deeper color.

**11** Mix 2 washes—1 of light orange for skin tone, the other light red for cheeks. Paint a small test patch of orange wash on a piece of white scrap paper. Let it dry. If the skin tone is too pale, add a little orange to the wash; if it is too orange, add water. Continue to test until you have the skin tone you like. Test the red wash in dabs on the orange wash until you have the right combination of skin tone and cheek coloring. Then cover the entire skin area of the doll

with the pale orange wash. Let this dry slightly (Fig. 8).

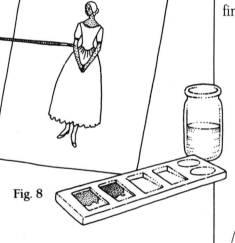

Fig. 8

**12** While the first wash is still damp, dab on the red wash for the cheeks. Let this dry.

**13** Choose a shading color—pale blue or gray wash—and paint as much detail as you want onto the face, using the finest brush (Fig. 9).

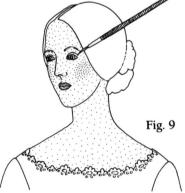

Fig. 9

**14** Complete your figure by painting in the hair, underwear, stockings, and shoes. A pencil helps to emphasize detail, and adds shading as well.

# Strengthening

× × × × × × × × × × × × × × × × × × × × × × × × × × × × × × × × × × × × × ×

**15** With the ruler, find the widest point on your figure—it should be somewhere toward the bottom of the petticoat. Using a soft pencil, draw a line down from this point to ¾ inch below the foot level on either side. Join these lines across the bottom (Fig. 10).

**Fig. 10**                    **Fig. 11**

**16** Using a matte knife and/or scissors, cut out along this line and cut around the rest of the body. Remember to cut out the spaces between the arms and the body, if these are drawn in as well (Fig. 11).

**17** Take the large sheet of balsa wood and lay your cutout paper silhouette on it. Using a soft pencil, trace around the shape onto the wood.

**18** Take the paper figure away and cover the traced wood area with a layer of rubber cement (Fig. 12).

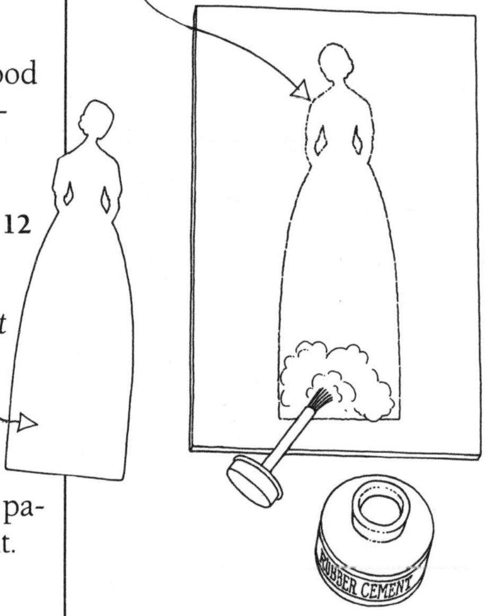

**Fig. 12**

*back of paper cutout*

**19** Cover the back of the paper figure with rubber cement. Let both dry.

**20** Lay the paper figure carefully and accurately, right side up, onto the balsa wood shape. Smooth it out very gently (Fig. 13).

**Fig. 13**

**21** This next stage is tricky. Lay the balsa sheet on a smooth cutting board, and making sure

*traced outline on balsa wood*

that your matte knife is really sharp, carefully cut the figure out of the balsa wood. Take extra care around the head, shoulders, and the space between the arms and the body.

**22** When you have cut it out, take a piece of fine sandpaper and gently rub the edges until they are smooth (Fig. 14).

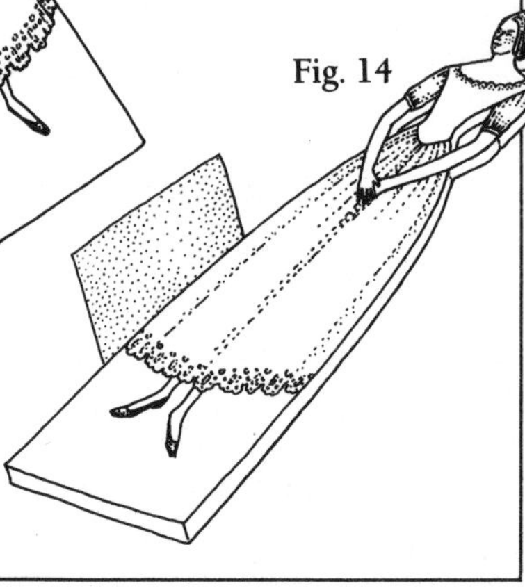

**Fig. 14**

# Making the Base

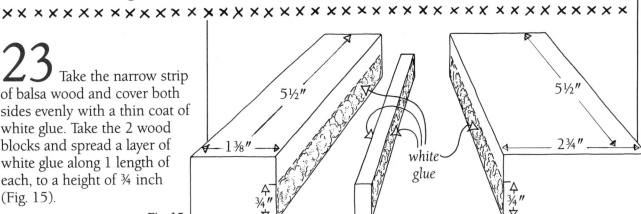

**23** Take the narrow strip of balsa wood and cover both sides evenly with a thin coat of white glue. Take the 2 wood blocks and spread a layer of white glue along 1 length of each, to a height of ¾ inch (Fig. 15).

**Fig. 15**

**24** Sandwich the balsa strip between the 2 glued wood blocks, making sure that the bottom edges are flush and that a groove is left between.

Wrap 2 strong rubber bands around the blocks to hold them securely. Let them dry (Fig. 16).

**Fig. 16**

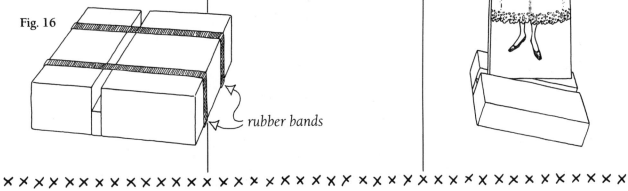

*rubber bands*

**25** Remove the rubber bands, and allow the glued block to stand for 1 hour. Then insert the base of the figure into the groove (Fig. 17).

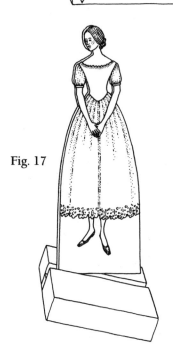

**Fig. 17**

# Making the Dress

Don't worry if you don't draw your dress perfectly at the first attempt. You can keep using layers of tracing paper until you are satisfied with the result. If you have placed the hands of your doll across the body, you will

have to re-draw them onto your dress design. This means that you can alter them if you like.

**26** Use the drawn silhouette you set aside in Step 10 as a guide for making the clothes. Place a piece of tracing paper over it, and draw in a dress you like, using your chosen picture as a model (Fig. 18).

**Fig. 18**

**27** Shade in the back of this tracing as you did for the body shape in Step 6.

**28** Take a piece of heavy-weight watercolor paper (it won't wrinkle too much when wet), and lay the traced dress over it. Tape down the corners with masking tape.

**29** Pencil around the dress, and check as you did before that you haven't left out any of the details. Remove the tracing, and emphasize the paper drawing with a hard pencil (Fig. 19).

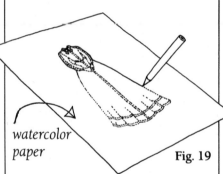

*watercolor paper*

**Fig. 19**

**30** Paint in the colors for the dress. When the paint is completely dry, cut the dress out (Fig. 20).

**Fig. 20**

# Hanging the Dress

Rather than making paper tabs, which break easily, I prefer to use white pipe cleaners or white garbage-bag ties.

**31** Cut 2 pieces of pipe cleaner long enough to stick to the dress shoulder and bend over the balsa figure to hold the dress securely.

**32** Using white glue, stick one end of each pipe cleaner just below each shoulder level on the back of the dress. (The tabs will be concealed when they are looped over the figure.) Now bend each tab and loop it over (Fig. 21).

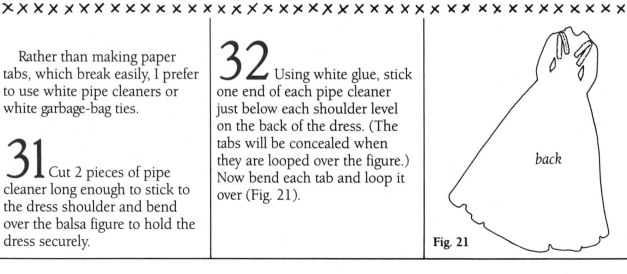

*back*

**Fig. 21**

# Adding a Hat

×××××××××××××××× ××××××××××××××× ××× ×××××××

## 33
Trace the head shape from your paper guide onto a piece of tracing paper. Draw any hat that you like onto this (Fig. 22).

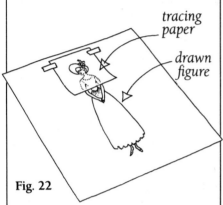

*tracing paper*

*drawn figure*

**Fig. 22**

## 34
Transfer it to heavy-weight watercolor paper as before: Shade the back with a soft pencil; trace onto the paper; emphasize the details; paint in the color and detail; and finally, cut it out around the entire circumference of the hat shape (Fig. 23).

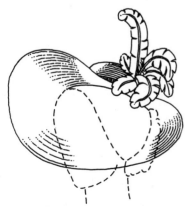

**Fig. 23**

## 35
Slit about halfway along the hat line with a matte knife. Now slip it onto the head and adjust if necessary (Fig. 24).

**Fig. 24**

## 36
If you have changed the hairstyle with your hat design, cut around the new hair shape and along the head contour (Fig. 25). You now have your own paper doll.

**Fig. 25**

# A Stocking Doll

**T**he method I have used to make my stocking doll is not the only one there is—but this kind is unusual in that it has a flat base, so there are no legs to make. I prefer to dress my stocking dolls in natural-fiber materials that look a bit worn whenever possible, as this really does enhance the handmade quality of the doll. I think it gives them a lovely, solid, down-to-earth quality.

## You Will Need

Scissors
1 pair flesh-colored panty hose or stockings
Tape measure
Pins
Dinner plate, 10 inches
Marking pen
Needles
Thread (an assortment)
Polyester stuffing
Pencil
Pearl or other buttons
Flesh-colored yarn
White glue
½ yard unbleached muslin, 1 yard wide

Pair of compasses
2 sheets thin (shirt) cardboard
Yarn for hair
Oil-based paints (brown, black, red, white)
Turpentine
Medium-size paintbrush
Heavy white typing paper
Brown wrapping paper
Yellow or blue carbon tracing paper
Tracing wheel
Heavy cardboard or matte board, 7½ inches square
Long-handled wooden spoon
Hat fabric, 18 inches square

Hat decoration (ribbon, lace, artificial flowers)
Bodice fabric, 7 x 3 inches
Skirt fabric, 30 x 11 inches
Lightweight apron fabric in light color, 12 x 7 inches
Waistband fabric or ribbon, 5 to 7 inches long
1 yard jacket fabric
1¼ yards bias binding tape (optional)
Orange watercolor paint (optional)
3 double-hole or other buttons (optional)
Lace fabric (optional)

# Making the Head

××××××××××××××××××××××××××××××××××××××××××

**1**  Cut both legs off the panty hose at their highest point (if you are using stockings, cut off the darker tops). Measure down 12 inches from the cut edge on both legs and cut again (Fig. 1). Discard the top and bottom pieces.

**Fig. 1**

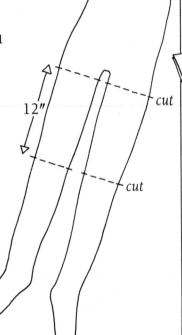

**2** Cut open both 12-inch pieces once lengthwise—or up the original back seam if there is one—and lay the pieces flat, one on top of the other (Fig. 2). Pin them together around the edges.

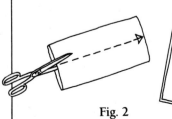

**Fig. 2**

**3** Take a 10-inch dinner plate and lay it over the material (making sure there is a complete circle of fabric beneath). Using your marking pen, draw around the plate onto the fabric, taking care not to pucker it (Fig. 3).

**Fig. 3**

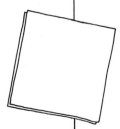

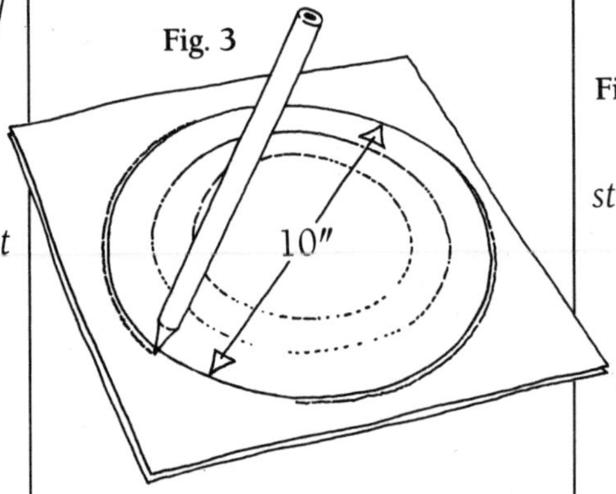

Remove the plate and pin the pieces together around the inner edge of the circle. Carefully cut out the circles.

**4** Using a double thread, stitch the two circles together with a running stitch around the edges, leaving a ¼-inch seam allowance. Be careful not to gather the material, but leave enough thread hanging in order to gather when you finish. Lay the circles on a flat surface.

**5** Take 2 handfuls of stuffing and place them in the middle of the stocking circle (Fig. 4). Then gently gather the thread until you have a pouch shape. Add more stuffing if necessary to make a solid, but not too tight, head shape (Fig. 5).

**Fig. 4**

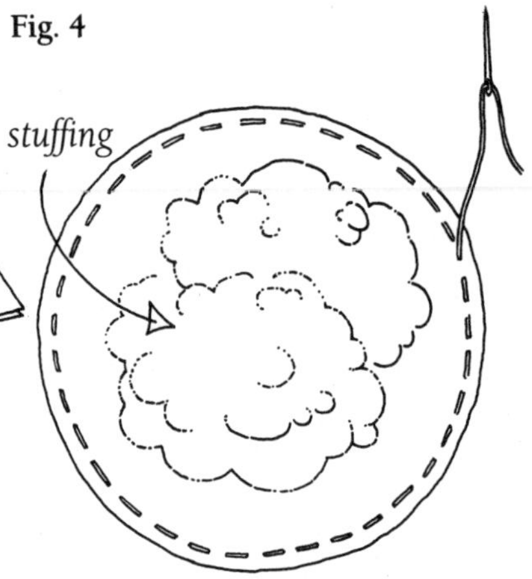

*stuffing*

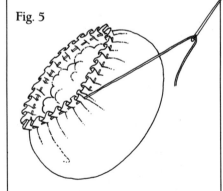

**Fig. 5**

**6** When the stuffing is complete, pull the gathering thread tight and close off the gap. Use an overcast stitch to strengthen and secure it.

# Quilting the Facial Features

**7** Take your stocking ball and flatten it into an oval shape. With a pencil, mark 2 dots for eyes, 2 dots for nostrils, and 2 dots for the corners of the mouth (Fig. 6).

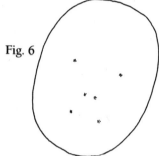

Fig. 6

**8** **The Eyes:** Thread a needle and knot the end so that there is a double strand. Bring the thread from the back of the head and through the center of the first eye-dot. Take it back again, leaving a small stitch. Pull the thread fairly tight so that you make a shallow indentation around the eye. Knot the stitch behind, and snip the thread. Re-peat the process for the other eye (Fig. 7).

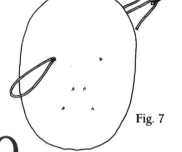

Fig. 7

**9** **The Nose:** Using the same procedure as for the eyes, make 2 small stitches at both nose-dots. You can add more, if you like, to make more detailed nostrils (Fig. 8).

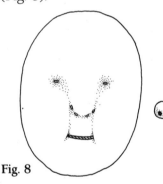

Fig. 8

**10** **The Mouth:** Again, use the same method, but with just one large stitch (Fig. 8).

**11** To complete the eyes, thread your needle as before, and bring it through the existing eye-stitch. Now attach one of your pearls (or buttons). Stitch this through, and secure at the back. Repeat for the other eye (Fig. 9).

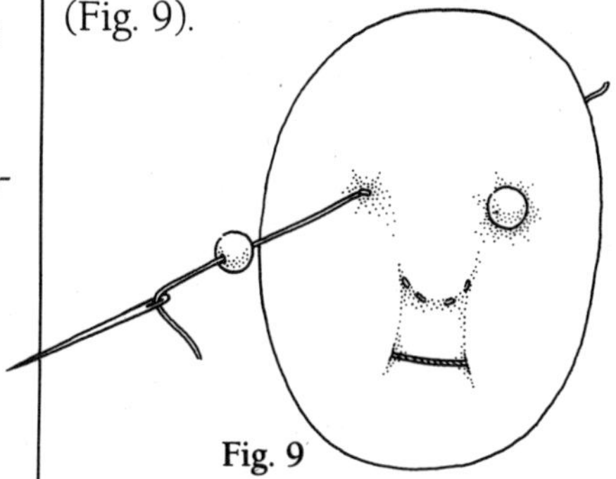

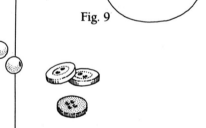

Fig. 9

# Adding Detail and Dimension

**12** **The Pupils:** A small circle of paper can be glued onto each pearl to give a pupil effect (Fig. 10).

Fig. 10

*paper circle*

**13** **The Eyelids:** Press a few short strands of yarn together and cover with glue. Then lay them, glue side down, over the tops of the pearl eyes. Let the glue dry (Fig. 11).

Fig. 11

# Preparing the Hair

**14** Cut a 7-inch circle out of unbleached muslin, using a pencil and compasses to mark the circle. Then measure in 2 inches, and draw a 5-inch circle onto the fabric (Fig. 12). Set the remaining muslin aside for now.

Fig. 12

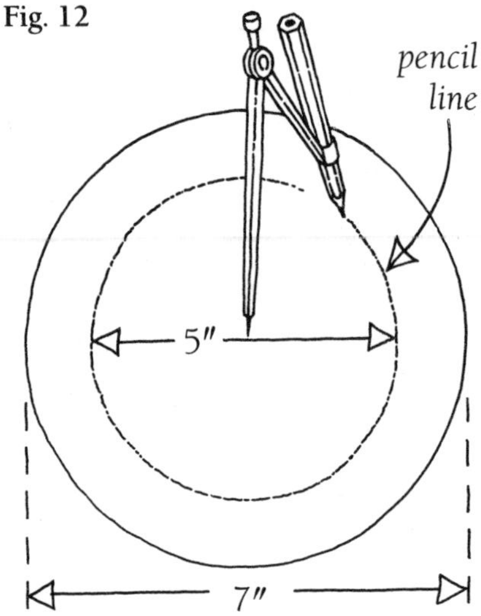

*pencil line*

5"

7"

**15** Now you should decide what length hair you would like. I usually allow about 8 inches, and to get this, I take a piece of thin cardboard, cut it to 8 x 4 inches, and wrap as much yarn as I can around it. Then I cut through it at one end. This saves having to cut a lot of single strands (Fig. 13).

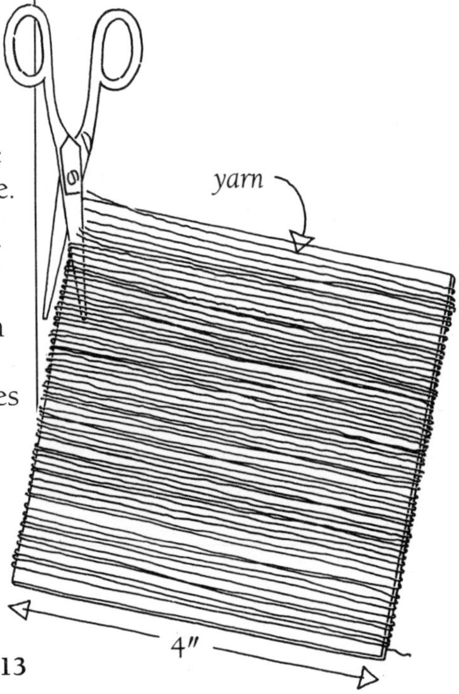

*yarn*

4"

**Fig. 13**

**16** Take a bunch of these strands, and pin one end onto the pencil line on your muslin circle. Then sew them onto the muslin, using about 4 small stitches. Continue this all around the 5-inch circle (Fig. 14). When you have finished, trim the ends off evenly.

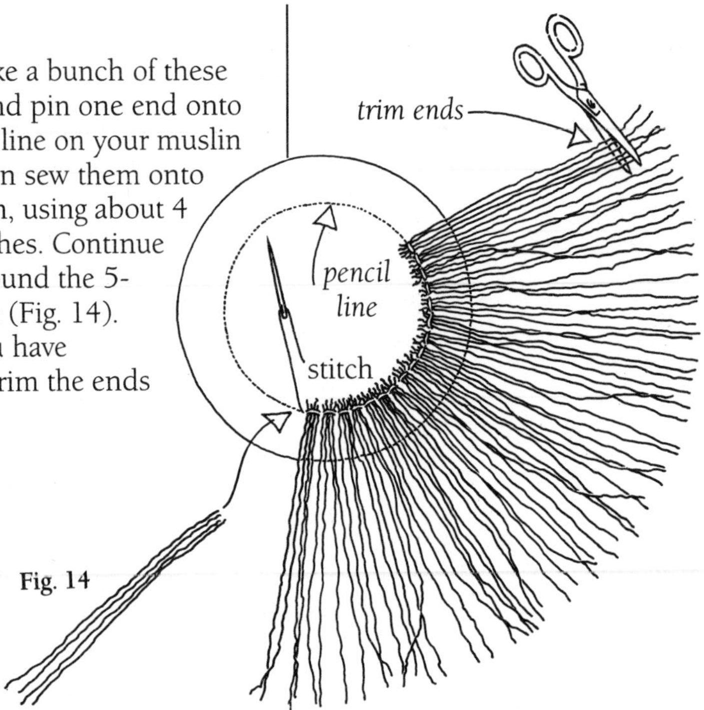

*trim ends*

*pencil line*

stitch

**Fig. 14**

**17** Turn the muslin over so that the hair is underneath, and make small, loose running stitches all along the outside edge. Then pull the thread to make a pouch shape similar to that of the face (Fig. 15).

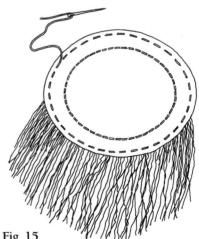

**Fig. 15**

**18** Fill this shape with stuffing, and pull the thread tight to close off the pouch (Fig. 16). Overcast the opening with several stitches to secure it.

Fig. 16

stuffing

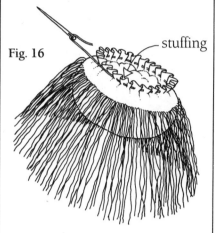

**19** Gather the hair lengths together, and tie them into a ponytail (Fig. 17).

Fig. 17

**20** Place the muslin side against the back of the stocking face, and pin them together in alignment. Then stitch together all the way around, using small overcast stitches (Fig. 18).

pin together

Fig. 18

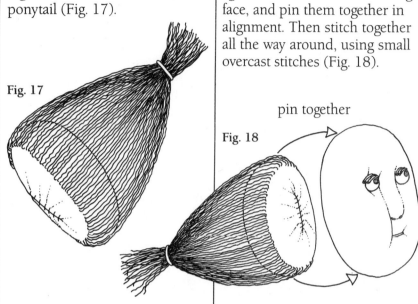

# Painting the Features

I like to finish the face at this stage—but if you wish, you could leave it until you have made the body. When adding features, be careful not to use too much paint as this will make the doll's face look heavy. It's a good idea to let the paint dry between stages. This takes a while, so don't rush to put more on. Use a small piece of leftover stocking and a bit of polyester stuffing to make a small stocking ball. Use it to test the paint colors before applying them to the face of your doll.

**21** Thin a little brown or black paint with turpentine, and paint the paper pupils, the eyebrows above the yarn eyelids, and a line around each whole eye (Fig. 19). Paint in some lashes around the eyes. Next, paint lightly around the nose to give it some definition (Fig. 20A).

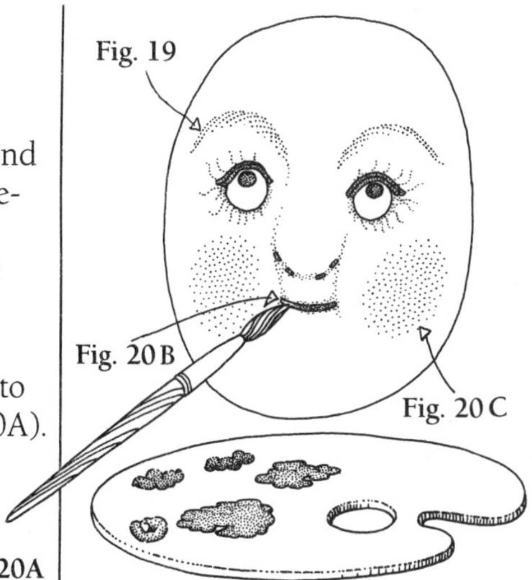

Fig. 20A

**22** Mix red and white paint and thin it with turpentine. Test the color on your small stocking ball. Adjust the mixture until you have a color you like, then use it to tint the mouth (Fig. 20B).

Fig. 19

Fig. 20 B

Fig. 20 C

**23** Thin the same pinkish mixture with a bit more turpentine and paint on the cheek coloring (Fig. 20C).

# Cutting Out the Body

✕ ✕ ✕ ✕ ✕ ✕ ✕ ✕ ✕ ✕ ✕ ✕ ✕ ✕ ✕ ✕ ✕ ✕ ✕ ✕ ✕ ✕ ✕ ✕ ✕ ✕ ✕ ✕ ✕ ✕ ✕ ✕✕ ✕ ✕ ✕ ✕ ✕ ✕ ✕ ✕ ✕

I find it a good idea to make these patterns in paper first, but if you feel confident, you can draw them straight onto the muslin.

**24** Inscribe a 7½-inch circle onto a piece of typing paper, using the pencil and compasses (Fig. 21).

**Fig. 21**

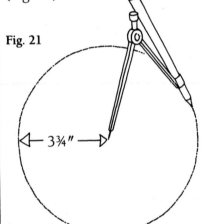

← 3¾″ →

**25** Draw the body shape, as shown, on a large piece of brown wrapping paper, and cut it out. Draw 2 arm shapes and cut them out (Fig. 22).

**Fig. 22**

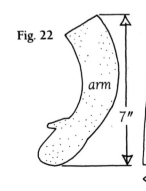

arm

7″

**26** Lay your unbleached muslin out flat, and fold it in half. Pin around the edges.

**27** Pin the paper patterns for the body and arms to the muslin following the grain of the fabric. Leave enough space between the patterns for a ½ inch seam allowance. Allowing for this width of seam, cut out the shapes. Open up the muslin and

8″

14″

body

10¾″

lay the circle pattern on a single layer. Pin the pattern to the muslin, and allowing an additional ½ inch all around, cut out the circle.

**28** Place the carbon paper between each pattern piece and the doubled muslin, with the carbon side facing the material, and trace around the paper patterns with the tracing wheel.

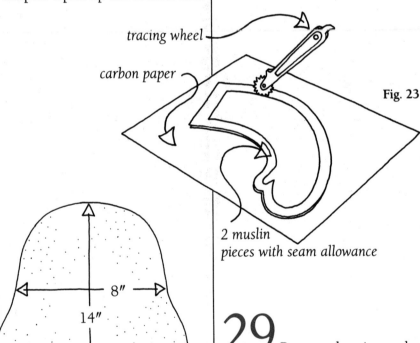

tracing wheel

carbon paper

**Fig. 23**

*2 muslin pieces with seam allowance*

**29** Remove the pins and paper patterns, and re-pin the muslin. Put the carbon under the unmarked side and repeat the procedure, tracing along the carbon line on the top side with the wheel (Fig. 23).

# Making Up the Body

**30** Cut out a 7½-inch circle of matte board or heavy cardboard for the base of the doll (Fig. 24).

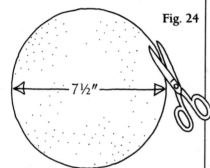

**Fig. 24**

7½″

**31** Leaving a ½-inch seam allowance, sew the muslin body pieces together using a small running stitch, from one bottom corner A to the other B (Fig. 25). Leave the bottom (straight) edge clear.

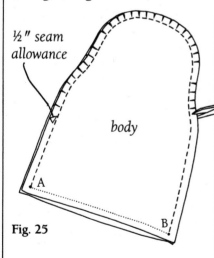

½″ seam allowance

body

A

B

**Fig. 25**

**32** Snip the seam allowance all around the body, snipping more closely together on the curve (Fig. 25).

**33** Take the circle-shaped muslin piece and pin it to the open end of the body shape, along the carbon lines. Pin only halfway around. Stitch together with running stitches (Fig. 26).

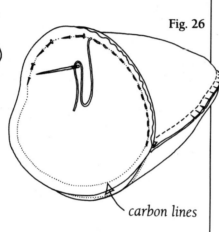

**Fig. 26**

carbon lines

**34** Turn the body shape right side out.

**35** Push some stuffing into the body through the opening, and pack it tightly with your wooden spoon handle until it is firmly packed.

**36** Keep filling until the stuffing reaches the opening. Then insert the matte board circle (Fig. 27). Finish by pushing in as much stuffing as you can.

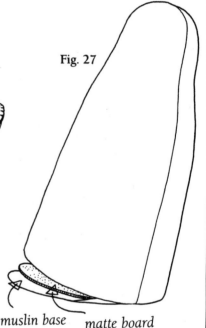

**Fig. 27**

muslin base     matte board

**37** To close the gap, fold the remaining seam allowance over the matte-board rim. Pin the gap shut, and stitch it up (Fig. 28).

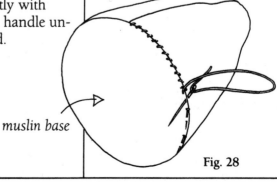

muslin base

**Fig. 28**

# The Arms

**38** Sew the 2 pieces of each arm together leaving a ½-inch seam allowance. Leave the shoulder end open. Snip the seam allowance. Turn the arms right side out.

**39** Fill each arm with stuffing to about 2 inches from the top. Using a running stitch, sew the arm closed along the A–B line (Fig. 29).

**40** Draw light pencil lines on the hands to mark the positions of the fingers. Sew small stitches along these lines to quilt the fingers (Fig. 30).

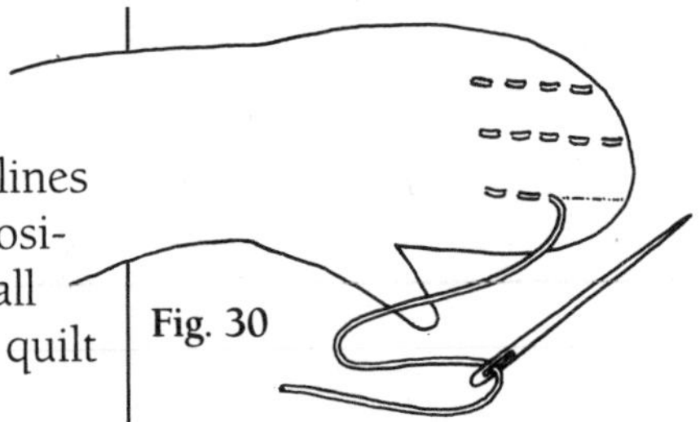

**41** Fold in ¼ inch of the loose end at the top of each arm and sew around the end with loose running stitches, pulling the thread through to gather (Fig. 31).

**42** Pin the gathered arm edge over the curve of the shoulder on the body shape, and stitch it down. Do the same with the other arm (Fig. 32).

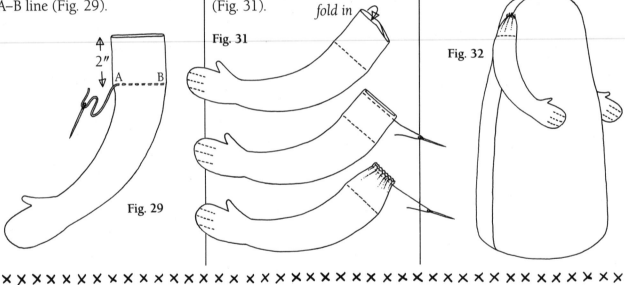

Fig. 30

*fold in*

Fig. 31

Fig. 32

2"

A     B

Fig. 29

# Attaching the Head

**43** Set the head onto the center of the body shape at the top. Pin the 2 shapes together and stitch, using small overcast stitches (Fig. 33).

Fig. 33

# Hair-Styling

x x x x x x x x x x x x x x x x x x x x x x x x x x x x x x x x x x x x x x x x x x x

By experimenting with the hair, you can create your own style, but if I am making a hat for my doll, I like to make a bun.

**44** Take the ponytail and twist the strands around until you have a loose knot shape—

rather like a bun. Pin this to the head and stitch securely (Fig. 34).

**Fig. 34**

x x x x x x x x x x x x x x x x x x x x x x x x x x x x x x x x x x x x x x x x x x x x

# Making a Hat

x x x x x x x x x x x x x x x x x x x x x x x x x x x x x x x x x x x x x x x x x x x x

**45** Cut a 7-inch circle out of light cardboard.

**46** Next, cut a 2-inch circle out of the center of this (Fig. 35).

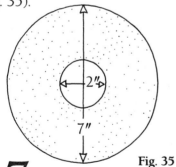

**Fig. 35**

**47** Take the fabric you chose for the hat, and using your cardboard circle as a template, mark and cut two 7-inch circles and one slightly larger (8-inch) circle.

**48** Cover the inner and outer ring edges of the cardboard circle on 1 side with white glue (Fig. 36).

**Fig. 36**

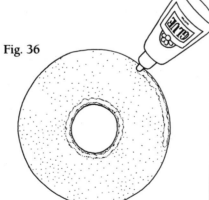

**49** Press this, glued side down, onto the wrong side of the 8-inch fabric circle. Let this dry.

**50** Snip the excess fabric all the way around (Fig. 37).

**Fig. 37**  *inner fabric circle*

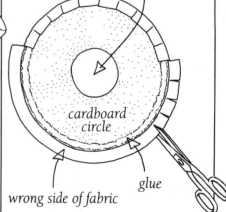

*cardboard circle*

*wrong side of fabric*  *glue*

**51** Put some glue around the edge of the cardboard circle, then press the snipped edge of the fabric firmly over it (Fig. 37).

**52** Coat the cardboard circle (including the turned-over fabric edge) with glue. Do not put glue on the inner fabric circle.

**53** Take one of the 7-inch fabric circles, and press it firmly onto the glued side of the card, right side out, as accurately as you can (Fig. 38).

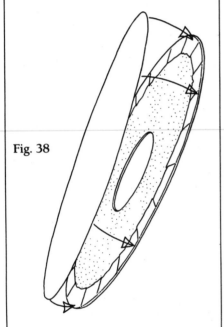

**Fig. 38**

**54** When it has dried, place this in position on the back of the doll's head. Secure by stitching the 2-inch center area of fabric to the head (Fig. 39).

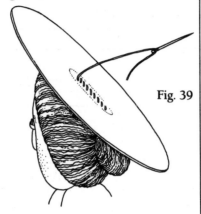

**Fig. 39**

**55** Take the other 7-inch circle of fabric and make a loose running stitch all around the edge. Pull it together slightly to make a pouch shape (Fig. 40). Fill this pouch shape lightly with stuffing.

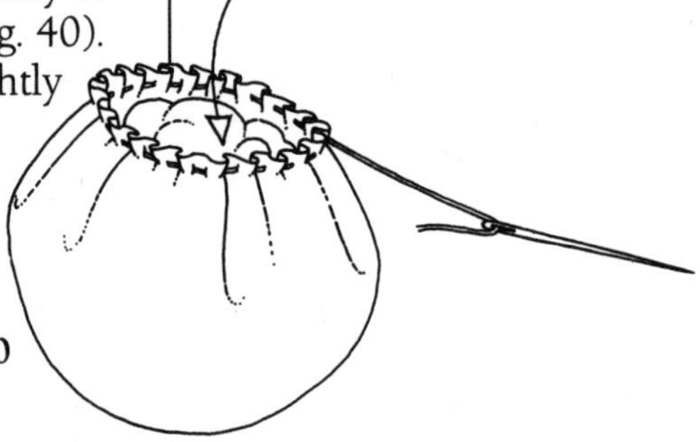

*stuffing*

**Fig. 40**

**56** Pull the thread to close the gap, and tie off.

**57** Pin the pouch to the center of the brim shape, and stitch it in place (Fig. 41). Add decorations such as ribbons, lace, or artificial flowers.

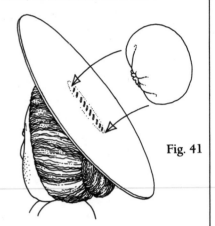

**Fig. 41**

# Creating a Bodice

**58** Lay the bodice fabric out flat. Cut a small semicircle, about 1 inch in diameter, from the center of the top length (Fig. 42).

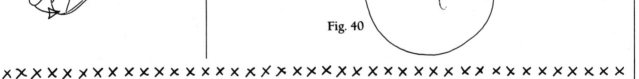

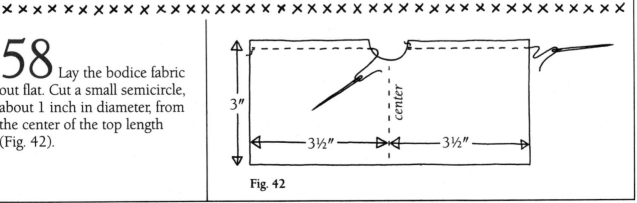

3″

3½″    *center*    3½″

**Fig. 42**

# 59
Stitch a row of loose running stitches close to the top edge, to the left and right of the semicircle.

Gather them until the length matches the width across the doll's shoulders, about 2½ inches on each side (Fig. 43).

# 60
Pin the whole piece of fabric onto the body, and stitch it right onto the doll (Fig. 44).

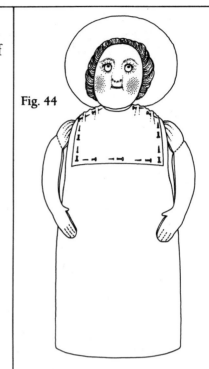

**Fig. 44**

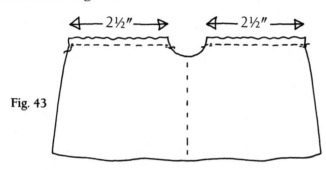

← 2½″ →          ← 2½″ →

**Fig. 43**

xxxxxxxxxxxxxxxxxxxxxxxxxxxxxxxxxxxxxxxxxxxxxxx

# Making the Skirt

xxxxxxxxxxxxxxxxxxxxxxxxxxxxxxxxxxxxxxxxxxxxxxx

# 61
Measure your doll's waist; it will be about 20 inches.

# 62
Take your piece of skirt fabric, make a 1-inch hem along 1 long edge, and stitch. (Leave this hem out if you want a "raggedy" look.)

# 64
Pin the skirt in place around the doll's waist and stitch it to the body, then turn in the edges and stitch up the back seam (Fig. 46).

**Fig. 46**

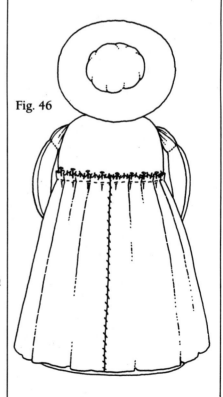

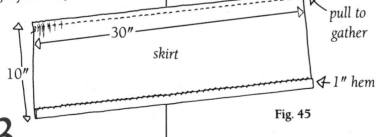

30″

*skirt*

10″

*pull to gather*

← 1″ hem

**Fig. 45**

# 63
Make a loose running stitch along the other length and gather it until you have the waist measurement (Fig. 45).

# Tying on the Apron

✕✕✕✕✕✕✕✕✕✕✕✕✕✕✕✕✕✕✕✕✕✕✕✕✕✕✕✕✕✕✕✕✕✕✕✕✕✕

**65** Use a piece of fabric 12 x 7 inches for the apron. Pin under ¼ inch around the 2 short sides and 1 long side of the apron fabric. Sew down the hem. Sew a loose running stitch along the unhemmed 12-inch length of the apron fabric. Pull the thread slightly to gather the apron.

**66** Pin this to the body at waist height, then stitch it on along the top edge (Fig. 47).

**Fig. 47**

✕✕✕✕✕✕✕✕✕✕✕✕✕✕✕✕✕✕✕✕✕✕✕✕✕✕✕✕✕✕✕✕✕✕✕✕✕✕✕✕

# Adding a Waistband

✕✕✕✕✕✕✕✕✕✕✕✕✕✕✕✕✕✕✕✕✕✕✕✕✕✕✕✕✕✕✕✕✕✕✕✕✕✕✕✕

**67** The waistband can be ribbon, braiding, or a piece of folded fabric 5 to 7 inches long. Pin the waistband onto the front waist area, covering the bottom edge of the bodice and the top edge of the apron (Fig. 48). Turn under the 2 short ends and pin.

**68** Slip-stitch this to the body along all 4 edges.

**Fig. 48**

# Making a Jacket

× × × × × × × × × × × × × × × × × × × × × × × × × × × × × × × × × × × × × × × ×

If you are quite experienced at sewing and are confident of your judgment, you could try making this without a paper pattern. Most people, however, prefer to use one.

**69** Following the measurements in Fig. 49, draw each pattern piece onto a sheet of brown wrapping paper and cut them out.

**Fig. 49**

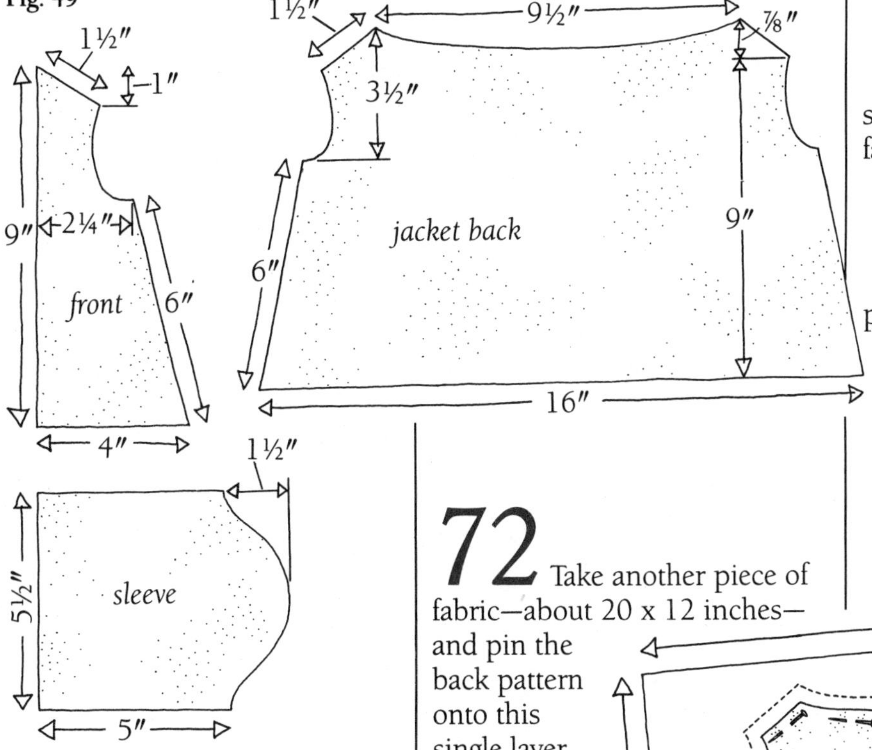

**70** Cut a piece of the jacket fabric to measure about 32 x 12 inches and lay it out flat on a smooth surface. Fold it in half and pin together around the edges.

**71** Lay the front and sleeve patterns onto this, leaving a ½-inch seam allowance around each pattern piece, and pin (Fig. 50).

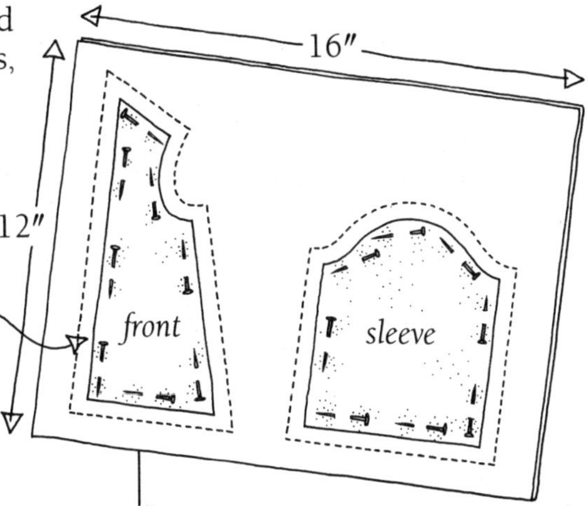

½" seam allowance

**Fig. 50**

**72** Take another piece of fabric—about 20 x 12 inches—and pin the back pattern onto this single layer (Fig. 51).

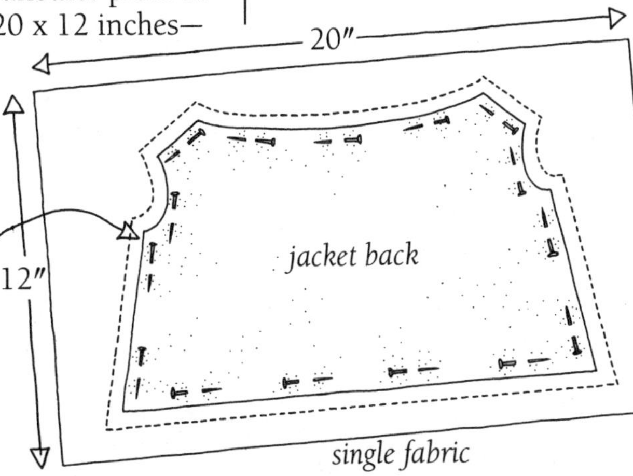

½" seam allowance

**Fig. 51**

single fabric

**73** Allowing ½ inch for seam allowances, cut out the fabric pattern pieces.

**74** Remove the paper patterns.

**75** Take the back piece and make a row of loose running stitches ½ inch down from the neck and shoulder edges, starting and finishing ½ inch in from each end (Fig. 52).

*start ½″ in*

*stop ½″ from edge*

*pull to gather*

*jacket back*

**Fig. 52**

**76** Gently pull the running stitches to gather until the top edge fits snugly across your doll's shoulders. Tie off the thread (Fig. 53).

*tie off when equal*

**Fig. 53**

**77** Pin the front and back pieces together, right sides facing, at the shoulders and the sides. Stitch the seams closed with a small running stitch, using a ½-inch seam allowance (Fig. 54).

**Fig. 54**

**78** Stitch each sleeve together along its side seam (Fig. 55).

**Fig. 55**

A

B

**Fig. 56**

**79** Run a loose running stitch along the capped edge of each sleeve from A to B, and gather it loosely (Fig. 56).

**80** Turn the sleeves right side out and pin each to the inside of each armhole—the gathered cap edge is at the top. Stitch it on (Fig. 57).

*wrong side of sleeve inside*

*wrong side*          **Fig. 57**

**81** Turn the jacket right side out. Roll or cut the sleeve to the length you like, leaving a raw edge or finish it with a hem.

# Finishing Touches

×××××××××××××××××××××××××××××××××××××××××

**82** Bias binding around the jacket edge gives a neat tailored finish (Fig. 58). Fit and pin one side of the bias binding to the inside of the jacket, around the front and neck edges. Do the same around the bottom edge, making sure any design in the binding matches up at the bottom front corners. (If you go around the edges of the jacket with one long piece of bias, simply pin a tuck into each of the front corners.) Slip-stitch around the edge to attach the binding. Secure the corner tucks (if you have made them) with an extra stitch. Fold and pin the bias binding over the front edges of the jacket. Slip-stitch the binding in place.

**Fig. 58**

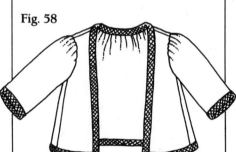

**83** Cut a small pocket shape out of fabric. Pin all the edges under ¼ inch. Sew the hem down with a loose running stitch (Fig. 59), then slip-stitch the pocket to the jacket.

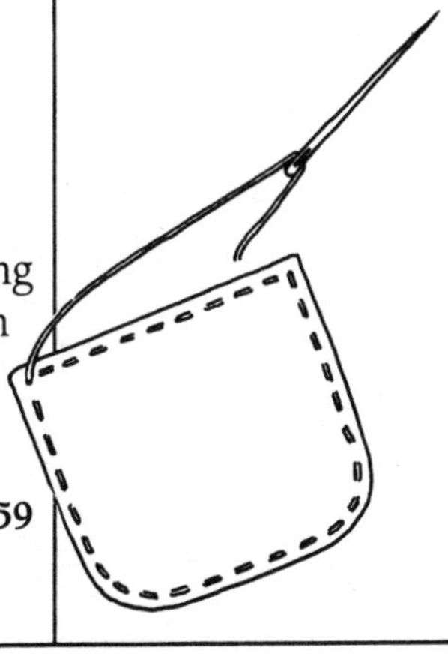

**Fig. 59**

**84** Give the doll's hands some color by wetting them with clear water and painting them with a light orange watercolor wash. (Test the color on a piece of scrap paper first.)

**85** If you wish, sew three buttons down the center front of the doll to finish off the bodice (Fig. 60).

**86** A sleeve of lace—from elbow to hand—can be stitched onto the doll's elbow to make a pretty false cuff (Fig. 60). Make a ruff for the neck from a different pattern of lace.

**Fig. 60**

**87** You now have your very own handmade stocking doll.

# A Papier-Mâché Doll

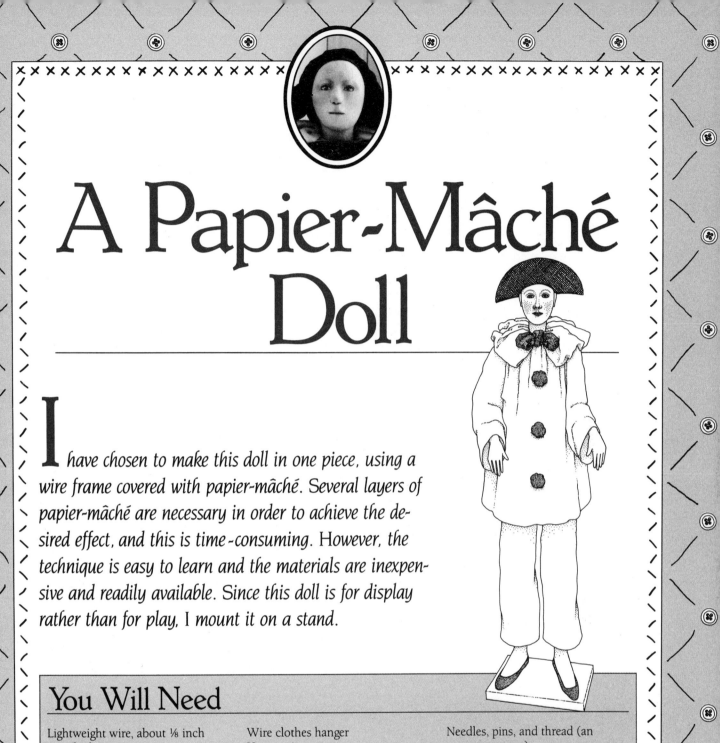

**I** have chosen to make this doll in one piece, using a wire frame covered with papier-mâché. Several layers of papier-mâché are necessary in order to achieve the desired effect, and this is time-consuming. However, the technique is easy to learn and the materials are inexpensive and readily available. Since this doll is for display rather than for play, I mount it on a stand.

## You Will Need

Lightweight wire, about ⅛ inch thick
Small pair of pliers
Plasticine
Newspaper
Tape (optional)
Wallpaper paste
Mixing bowl
Water
White tissue paper
Scissors
Pencil
Matte knife
Spoon
Block of wood, 4 x 4 x ½ inch

Wire clothes hanger
Heavy wire cutter
Old towel
Plaster of paris
Knife
Gesso (optional; available from art-supply stores)
Fine sandpaper (optional, for gesso)
Acrylic paints (flesh-tone, white, red, and various colors for the face)
Paintbrushes (medium and fine)
White scrap paper
Tape measure
2½ yards white cotton fabric

Needles, pins, and thread (an assortment)
Steam iron
Strip of lace or net, 24 x 4 inches, or other lightweight fabric
White glue
Small piece of cardboard
½ yard black velvet, 36 inches wide
1 yard satin ribbon, 2 to 3 inches wide
Old black sock (optional)
Black felt, 20 x 10 inches
Wood drill
Thick elastic bands

# Making the Body Frame

You can use 1 length of wire to make the whole figure. Experiment with bending, twisting, and coiling a piece of the wire first; the pliers may be useful here.

**1** Take the wire and bend it over 12 inches from 1 end—this is the head-to-waist length. Twist the wires together 5 inches from the top to form a noose shape; this forms the head and neck (Fig. 1).

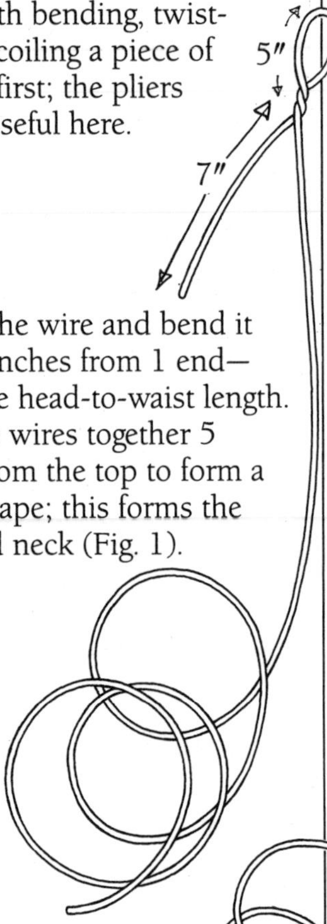

**Fig. 1**

**2** About 27 inches down from the neck, bend the wire up—this is the full extension of the leg. Bring the wire up and twist the wires together at hip level. Loop it down again, and form the other leg in the same way (Fig. 2).

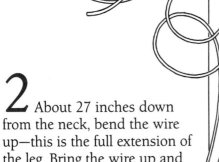

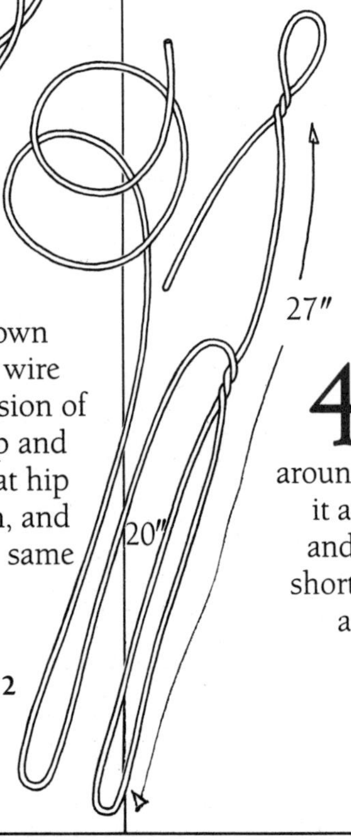

20″

27″

**Fig. 2**

**3** Twist the wires together at the bottom of each leg, creating a noose shape for each foot. Twist the wires halfway up the leg to form the knees (Fig. 3).

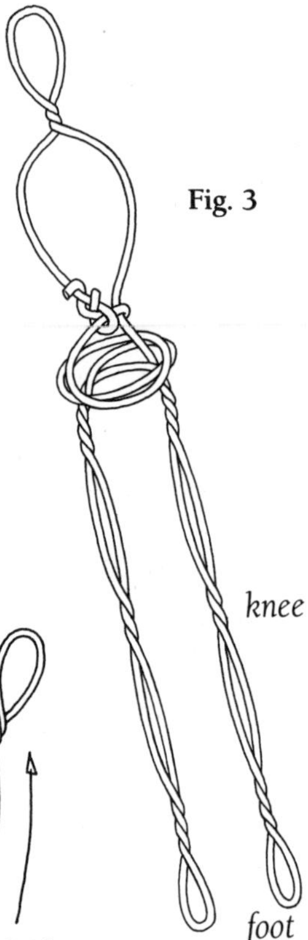

**Fig. 3**

knee

foot

**4** Circle the wire around the hips, twist it around the waist, and incorporate the short wire end in the armature (Fig. 3).

**5** You can continue with this wire, or if you find it too unwieldy, cut it with pliers and use a separate length to make the arms. To form the arms, loop the wire over to form a 12-inch length for each arm, and twist the wires together, as you did for the legs, making noose shapes for the hands. Twist the wires together to form the elbows, and twist the ends of the wire around the shoulders to anchor it (Fig. 4).

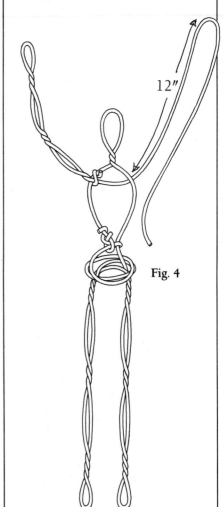

12″

**Fig. 4**

5″

7″

**6** Bend the foot loops at the ankle joints to enable the figure to stand (Fig. 5).

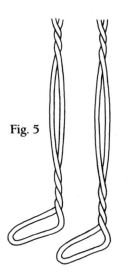

**Fig. 5**

**7** Take some Plasticine and mold a clay foot over each wire shape, extending about 3 inches from the heel point up the leg. Make sure that the sole of each foot is flat (Fig. 6).

**Fig. 6**

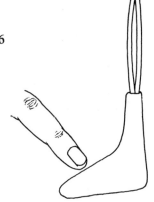

**8** This is the time to bend your wire figure into the position you want (Fig. 7)

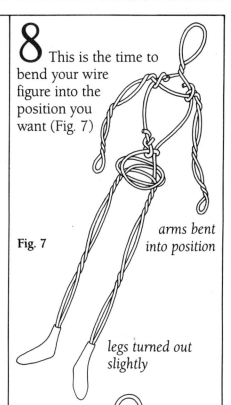

**Fig. 7**

*arms bent into position*

*legs turned out slightly*

# ×××××××××××××××××××××××××××××××××××××××××××××
# Applying Papier-Mâché
# ×××××××××××××××××××××××××××××××××××××××××××××

Papier-mâché is time-consuming because of the drying time required. If the weather is warm and dry, the process goes faster. Humid weather will slow you down.

You will probably find your own way of applying the paste and paper. To get it all well saturated, I dip my hand in the mixed paste, spread it all over the figure, and lay on the paper strips. Then I paste over the strips by hand, and proceed layer by layer.

**9** To make a good, bulky base, tear some long strips of newspaper, 3 to 4 inches wide, and crush them loosely lengthwise. Wrap these around the body area of the wire frame. Keep them in place by pushing the ends in between the wires, or attach them with small strips of tape (Fig. 8).

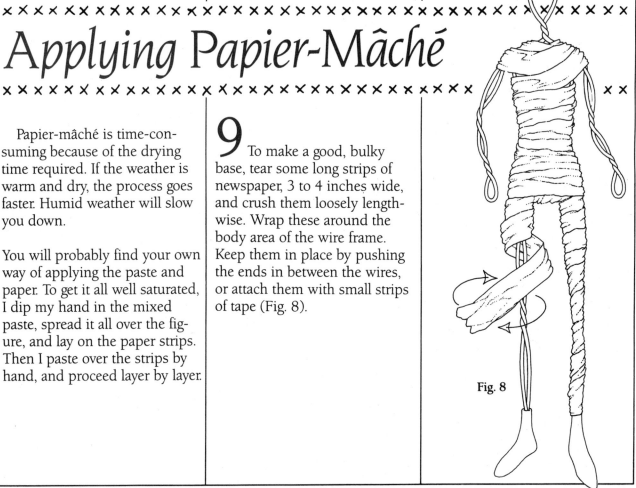

**Fig. 8**

**10** Continue doing this down the legs to the ankles, and over the arms and hands—but use less volume of paper there. Wrap some around the head. Try to make the bulk proportional to the shape of the body.

**11** Mix the wallpaper paste in the bowl following the instructions on the package (Fig. 9), but use slightly less water to make it thicker. Tear newspaper into small, narrow strips.

**Fig. 9**

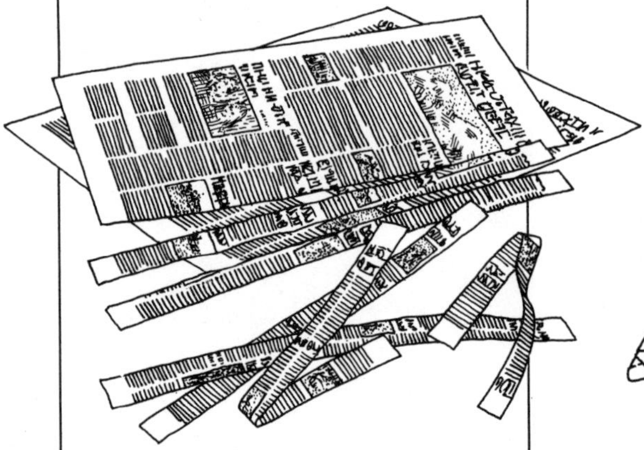

**12** Cover the figure with wallpaper paste, and then lay the small strips all over it. Cover these with more paste, followed by another layer of strips. Make sure that all these are covered with paste, then leave the figure in a warm place to dry overnight (Fig. 10).

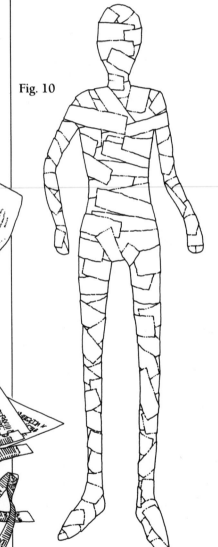

**Fig. 10**

**13** Repeat the paste and newspaper process—about 3 more layers—and leave the figure to dry overnight each time.

**14** Tear tissue paper into strips and apply a final covering of paste and paper with these. (Fig. 11).

**Fig. 11**

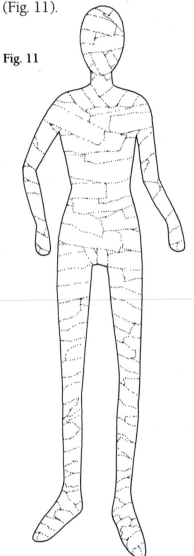

**15** Now you can build up some body detail and dimension on your figure, such as in the chest and hip areas, the buttocks and the calf muscles. Make small bunches of tissue and stick them in place by covering them with pasted tissue strips.

# Fine Details

×××××××××××××××××××××××××××××××××××××××××××××××

**16** Once you have made a good oval face shape, make a small roll of tissue for the nose. Stick it in place, and paste small tissue strips over it (Fig. 12).

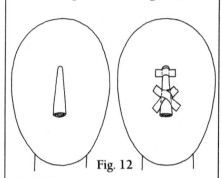

Fig. 12

**17** Fold a small piece of tissue several times and lay it across the head to build up the forehead. Paste tissue strips over it to secure it (Fig. 13).

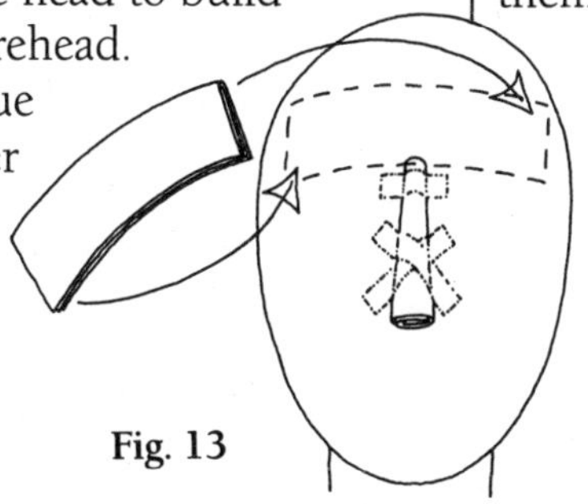

Fig. 13

**18** Make 2 small oval shapes, not quite flat, and paste them in place for the eyes (Fig. 14).

Fig. 14

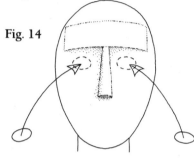

**19** Make a small half-triangle wad for the upper-lip area, and a small oval wad for the lower lip (Fig. 15). Paste them in place.

Fig. 15

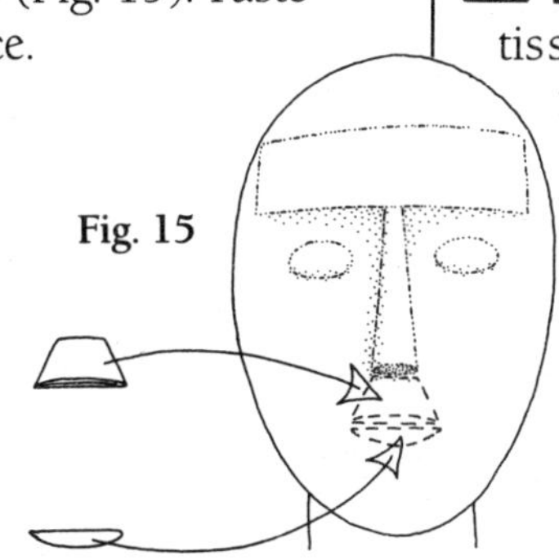

**20** Add flat circular wads for the chin and each cheek. Then make ear-shaped wads and add these (Fig. 16).

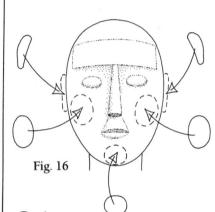

Fig. 16

**21** Lay on more strips of tissue until all the features are reasonably smooth and regular.

×××××××××××××××××××××××××××××××××××××××××××××××

# The Hands

×××××××××××××××××××××××××××××××××××××××××××××××

**22** Roll 10 pasted tissue strips to form tubes roughly 1 inch long. Stick them in place on each hand (Fig. 17) and lay pasted tissue strips across to cover the joins. Let them dry overnight.

Fig. 17

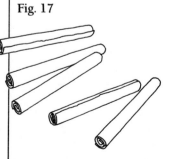

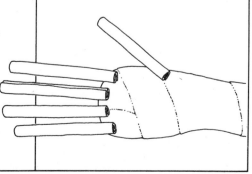

**23** When the fingers are dry, use scissors to snip them to their correct lengths (Fig. 18): The middle one is the longest, the 2 on either side of it are of equal length, and the little finger and thumb are in proportion to these (check your own hands as a guide). Cover both hands with a final layer of pasted tissue strips. Try to make the fingertips as round as possible (Fig. 19).

**24** Allow the figure to dry *completely*—overnight.

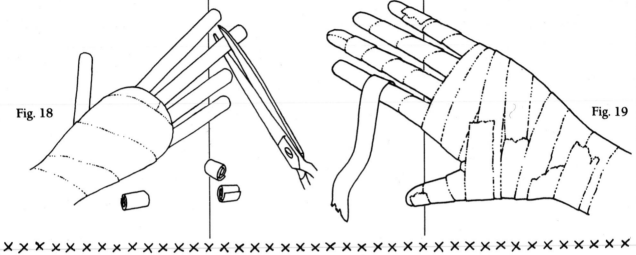

Fig. 18

Fig. 19

# Making the Foot Prongs

**25** When the figure is thoroughly dry, sketch a line around the edge of the sole of each foot. Cut around this with a matte knife, and remove the soles (Fig. 20).

**26** With a spoon, scoop out as much of the Plasticine inside as you can (Fig. 21).

**27** Place the feet on the block of wood and pencil their outlines onto the wood (Fig. 22).

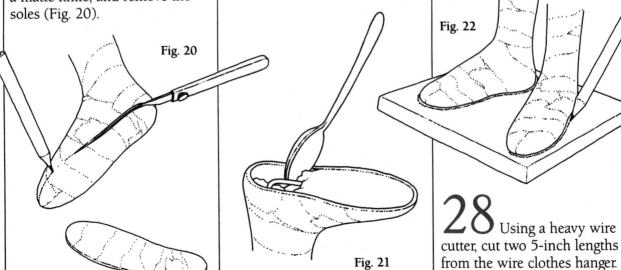

Fig. 20

Fig. 21

Fig. 22

**28** Using a heavy wire cutter, cut two 5-inch lengths from the wire clothes hanger. Bend the wire pieces in half.

# The Dollmaking Collection

# Simple
# Rag Dolls (page 13)

A collection of early American homespun fabrics, combined with a fascination for primitive American Indian dolls, was the inspiration for these dolls. I find the simplicity of their flat silhouette shapes very beautiful. The visible overcast stitching enhances the handmade feeling and also blends perfectly with the texture of the fabric from which the dolls are made.

# Dressed Rag Doll (page 21)

Rag dolls have no pretentions. For me they represent the earthy, grass-roots quality that is so much a part of American history. They are easy to construct and can be made from almost any scrap of cloth available. Once constructed, they are also sturdy enough to be played with and loved by children for many years. The wear and tear seems to improve them.

## Paper Doll (page 35)

Most paper dolls have an ephemeral quality about them, a feeling of non-permanence, but that needn't be the case. Years ago I discovered a way of backing the dolls with balsa wood and constructing a stand for them, making them easier to play with and more durable. Once completed they can also be used as display pieces on a tabletop or book shelf.

# Stocking Doll (page 43)

The flesh-like quality of stocking material and the ease with which a stitch here and there gives this doll its own individual character, make these dolls accessible even to dollmakers with little experience. You don't need to know how to sculpt in order to create some unique and very funny faces.

# Papier-Mâché Doll (page 59)

Papier-mâché is a technique that most people learn in grade school. Newspaper, wheat paste, and wire are inexpensive materials to acquire, and the finished results can be very effective. These dolls can be constructed in all shapes and sizes and make wonderful pieces for display.

## Clay Doll (page 73)

This young mid-Victorian woman was made from one of the popular craft clays that bake easily in a kitchen oven and require no plaster molds. The clay allows the dollmaker to achieve great detail and the technique is straightforward. Even if you are a timid sculptor, you should give it a try. You'll find your confidence and your sculpting skills will improve with each doll.

# Wax Doll (page 87)

Working with wax is time consuming and difficult until you get the knack of it. It is worth the effort, however, as no other material has the same translucent properties that make a wax doll unique. Expect mistakes and persevere. The finished doll will bring a great sense of achievement.

**29** Wrap the figure in an old towel, and wedge it upside down between 2 piles of books. Mix up a little plaster of paris, fairly thick, and pour it into the foot cavities (Fig. 23). As it starts to set, push the bent end of 1 of the wire prongs into each foot, leaving at least 1 inch exposed beyond the heel (Fig. 24).

**30** Smooth the soles flat with a knife so that they are flush with the edge (Fig. 24). Let the plaster of paris dry (5 to 10 minutes).

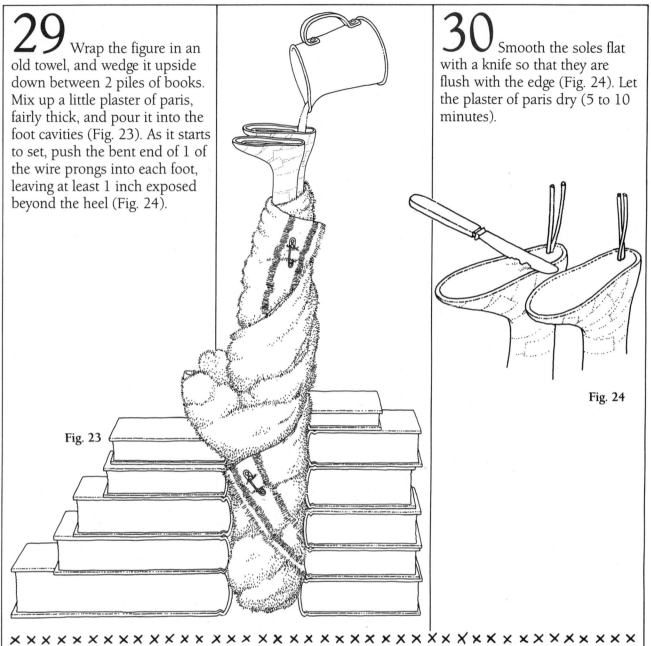

Fig. 23

Fig. 24

# Refining and Painting

Acrylic paints dry fast, so you will need to work quickly when you are painting the features and details. For this doll, you might like to paint on a full clown's makeup—or perhaps a half-mask. If so, follow an illustration as you work.

**31** If you want to refine the face, or if you feel the surface of the face is not smooth enough, paint a layer of gesso over it.

When the gesso has dried, sand it down to a smooth finish. (Gesso is helpful for covering up mistakes or improving what you have already done.)

## 32

For the foundation face color, start with a flesh-tone paint and mix it with white. Test it on a sheet of white paper until the color suits you. Then paint the face and hands, using a medium-size brush. While the paint is still wet, add color to the cheeks: mix red with some orange, dab it on, and blend it in. Let this dry before you paint the rest of the face (Fig. 25).

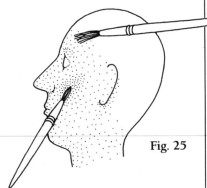

**Fig. 25**

## 33

Using a fine brush and a pale flesh-tone/orange mixture, paint in the lips.

## 34

Color the eyes blue or brown (Fig. 26A). Mix a light

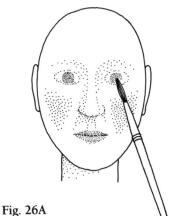

**Fig. 26A**

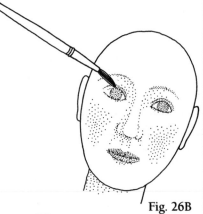

**Fig. 26B**

gray or brown paint and use it to shade the eyelids. Sketch in the eyebrows with a pencil. With the fine brush, paint over the eyebrow pencil line. A thin, arched eyebrow looks good on this doll. Use a fine brush to define the line around the eyelids (Fig. 26B).

## 35

Paint in the pupils of the eyes, and, when they are dry, add a white dot (Fig. 27).

**Fig. 27**

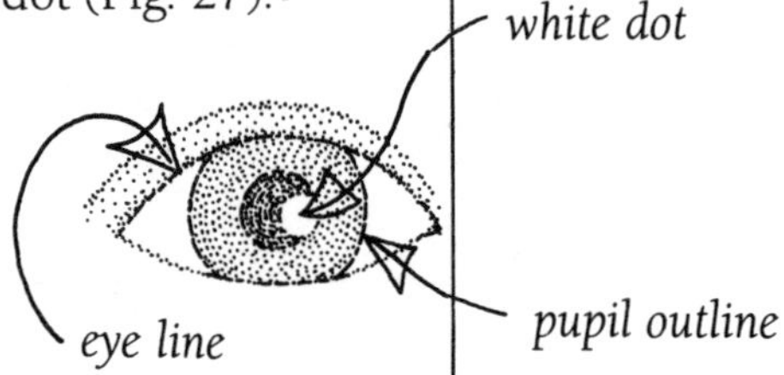

*white dot*

*eye line*

*pupil outline*

## 36

Add a little brown to some red paint, and lightly paint a line between the lips to define the mouth. Use this color to indicate the nostrils as well (Fig. 28).

## 37

Place a dot of pale red paint in the inner corner of each eye.

## 38

Sketch the outline of a slip-on shoe on each foot. Paint white stockings onto the legs, and a black shoe onto each foot (Fig. 29).

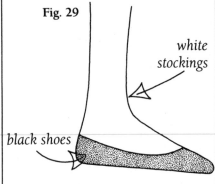

**Fig. 29**

*white stockings*

*black shoes*

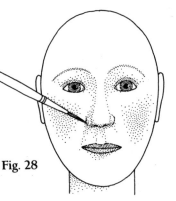

**Fig. 28**

# Hair

× × × × × × × × × × × × × × × × × × × × × × × × × × × × × × × × × × × × × × × × × × ×

I do not make hair for this doll, since the hat will cover its head. If you want hair, follow the method described for the Clay Doll (page 81).

× × × × × × × × × × × × × × × × × × × × × × × × × × × × × × × × × × × × × × × × × × ×

# The Costume

× × × × × × × × × × × × × × × × × × × × × × × × × × × × × × × × × × × × × × × × × × ×

**39** Measure from the base of the neck to midthigh on your figure—here it is 13 inches. If necessary, adjust the fabric dimensions to fit your figure. Cut out:

2 pieces of white cotton fabric, 16 x 14 inches each (bodice)
2 pieces of white cotton fabric, 10 x 9 inches each (sleeves)
2 pieces of white cotton fabric, 17 x 15 inches each (pants)

**40** Lay 1 bodice piece on top of the other, right sides facing, and pin them together. Mark the center front point. Stitch ½-inch seams along the 2½-inch lines A–B and C–D. Then stitch ½-inch side seams along the 10-inch lines E–F and G–H. This will leave holes for the head, arms, and waist (Fig. 30).

**41** Fold the sleeve pieces in half lengthwise, right sides facing. Pin and stitch up a ½-inch seam for each sleeve (Fig. 31).

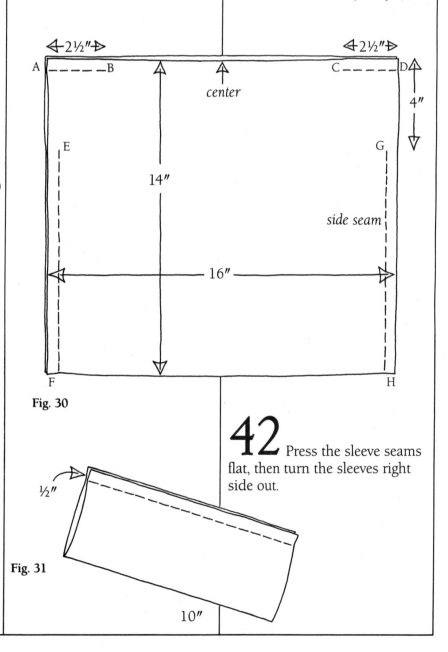

**Fig. 30**

**Fig. 31**

**42** Press the sleeve seams flat, then turn the sleeves right side out.

**43** Lay both sleeves inside the bodice and pin them to the armholes. Stitch around a ½-inch seam (Fig. 32). Press the seams flat, then turn the bodice right side out.

**45** Pin ½-inch side seam allowances and stitch closed C–D and H–G. Stitch along the pencil line E–B–F.

**49** Place the pants in position on your figure, and pull the gathering until they fit around the waist. Stitch over to secure, and tie off (Fig. 35).

**44** Take the 2 pieces of fabric for the pants and pin them together, right sides facing. Mark the top center point A, then measure down 6 inches and mark B. Measure 5½ inches in from each corner along the bottom edge, and mark E and F. Draw an arch shape from E to B to F. Cut out along a line ½ inch in from this (Fig. 33).

**46** Snip the seam allowance around E–B–F.

**47** Press the seams flat, and turn the pants right side out.

**48** Turn ½ inch under around the top edge, and pin. Make a gathering stitch along this edge (Fig. 34).

**50** Pin a similar ½-inch hem around the neckline of the bodice and make a gathering stitch.

inside-out sleeve

bodice

Fig. 32

Fig. 35

Fig. 33

Fig. 34

**51** Put the bodice on the figure, and pull the gathering to close around the neck. Stitch to secure, and tie off (Fig. 36).

*pull to gather*

**Fig. 36**

**52** Turn up the hems on the sleeves, bodice, and pants to the lengths you like, and hem-stitch around.

**53** To make a ruff, hem a strip of lightweight fabric all around, or use a strip of lace or net, so you have a finished strip that measures 24 x 4 inches. Make a gathering stitch along one length, and pull to gather (Fig. 37).

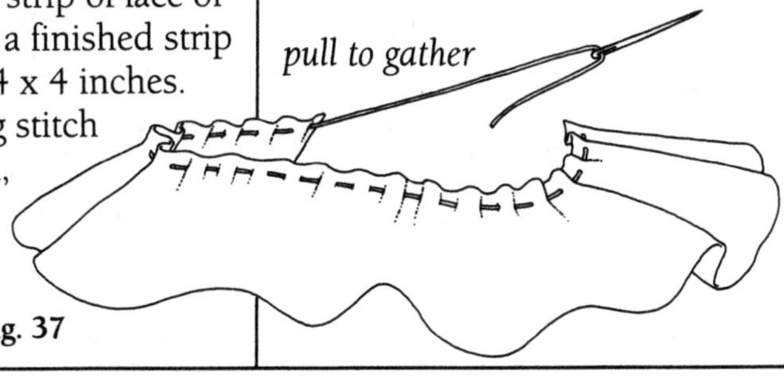

*pull to gather*

**Fig. 37**

**54** Place the strip around the neck, and gather until it fits. Stitch to secure, and either stitch the ends together or leave them open. To fix it permanently, paste the inner edge of the ruff to the papier-mâché with white glue.

**55** **The Buttons:** Cut 3 circles measuring 1¼ inches in diameter out of cardboard, then 3 circles 2½ inches in diameter out of velvet. Run a gathering stitch around the outside edge of the pieces of velvet (Fig. 38A).

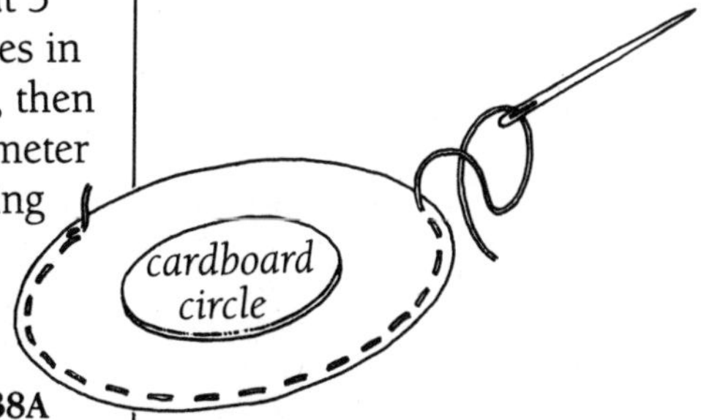

*cardboard circle*

**Fig. 38A**

**56** Place each cardboard circle on the wrong side of a velvet circle. Pull the gathers tightly over the cardboard (Fig. 38B). Tie off the thread. Pin the velvet buttons in place on the bodice front, and stitch them in place (see finished doll).

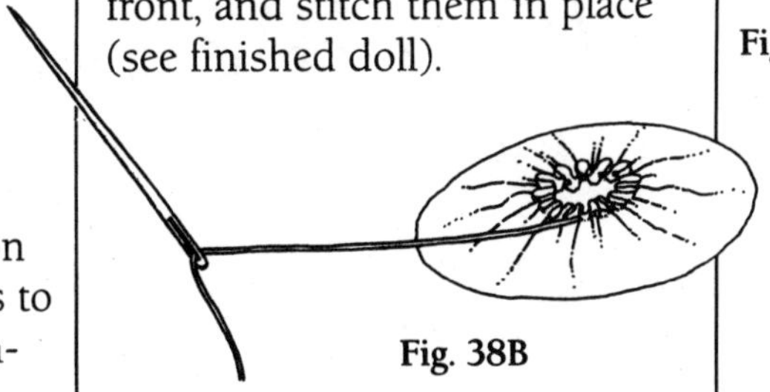

**Fig. 38B**

**57** **The Bow:** Cut a length of 2- or 3-inch-wide satin ribbon to a length of 12 to 15 inches. Tie it in a simple bow, pin it to the bodice neck, and stitch it in place. Trim the ribbon end to the desired length.

**58** **The Hat:** First, make a skullcap: If you have an old black sock, snip off the toe and glue it smoothly onto the head. Alternatively, paint the top of the head black (Fig. 39).

**Fig. 39**

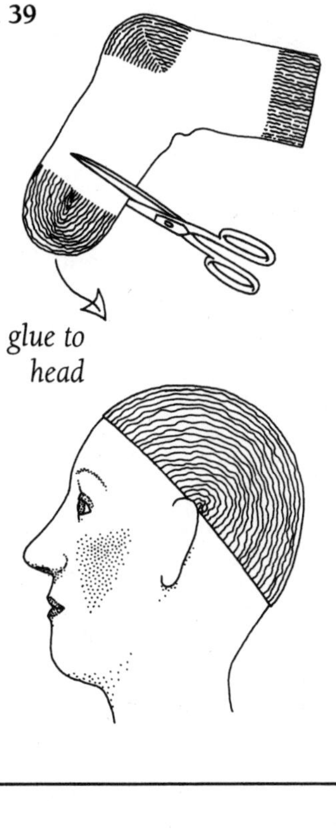

*glue to head*

**59** Cut 2 circles measuring 8 inches in diameter out of black felt. Stick them together with white glue, evenly spread. Measure the doll's head around the skullcap, then use a compass to draw a circle the same size in the center of the black felt brim. Cut out the circle so the brim fits snugly over the skullcap (Fig. 40).

*fold up to meet*

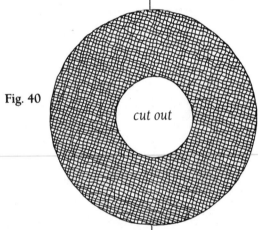

**Fig. 41**

**Fig. 40**

*cut out*

**60** Press the felt brim onto the head at an angle. Pull up the front and back edges to meet. Attach them at the center with white glue or with a couple of small invisible stitches (Fig. 41).

# Fixing the Doll to the Mount

**61** Using a drill bit the right size to hold the wire foot prongs, drill a hole through the block of wood at the center heel point in the drawn outline of each foot (Fig. 42).

*drill holes*

**62** Push the foot prongs through these holes, and mark the point on each wire that is flush with the bottom of the block (Fig. 43).

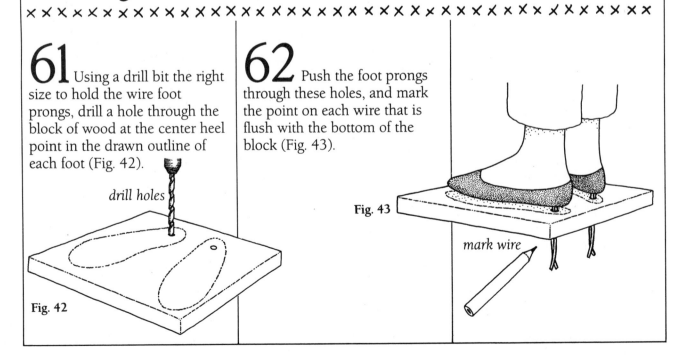

**Fig. 43**

*mark wire*

**Fig. 42**

# 63

Pull the prongs out of the wood blocks and snip the wire at those marks (Fig. 44).

**Fig. 44**

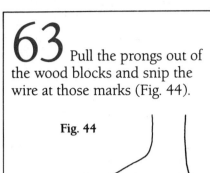

# 64

Cover the exposed wire and the drawn foot shapes on the block with white glue. Place the prongs back in the holes, and press the feet carefully but firmly into place. A thick elastic band around the block and feet will help to hold them in position (Fig. 45). Allow the glue to dry thoroughly before removing the bands.

*elastic bands*

**Fig. 45**

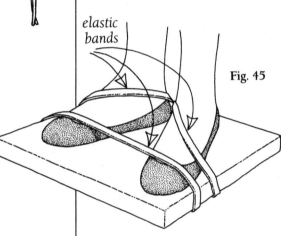

# 65

You now have your own papier-mâché doll.

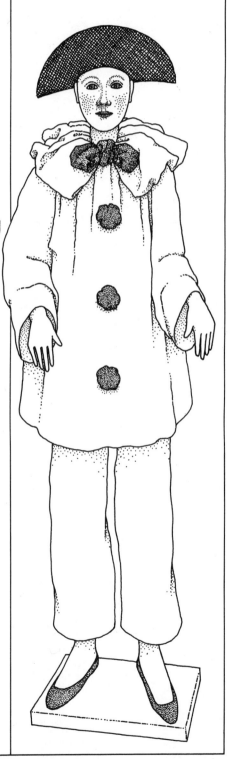

# A Clay Doll

**T**his doll can be modeled with a simple sculpting tool directly from a craft clay that can be fired in a normal kitchen oven. The head and shoulders, hands and feet are made from clay. The body is made from cloth.

## You Will Need

Package of craft clay, such as Sculpey or Super Sculpey that fires at a low or medium kitchen oven temperature
Tape measure
Kitchen knife
Modeling tools (available from art supply stores): 6-inch wire-end modeling tool, 6-inch wood modeling tool
Pencil
Baking sheet (to bake the clay)

Acrylic paints (flesh-tone, white, red, blue, black, and brown)
Paintbrushes (medium-size and fine)
White scrap paper
Brown wrapping paper
Scissors
1 yard unbleached muslin
Pins
White glue
Needle and thread (an assortment)
Kapok stuffing

Hair (mohair, crepe or wool yarn, embroidery thread or an old wig)
1 yard cotton fabric
Steam iron
Facing
3 small buttons
Embroidery thread
Scrap bag for trimmings and accessories

# Modeling the Head

✗ ✗ ✗ ✗ ✗ ✗ ✗ ✗ ✗ ✗ ✗ ✗ ✗ ✗ ✗ ✗ ✗ ✗ ✗ ✗ ✗ ✗ ✗ ✗ ✗ ✗ ✗ ✗ ✗ ✗ ✗ ✗ ✗ ✗ ✗ ✗ ✗ ✗ ✗ ✗ ✗

Most clays need to be softened before you start. Cut the clay into manageable chunks with a kitchen knife. Take a small amount and rub and roll it between the palms of your hands. Once it is pliable, you can begin. The height of the entire head and shoulder piece for the doll is 3½ inches. The width from shoulder to shoulder is 4 inches. The head and neck should be about two-thirds of the entire 3½-inch height.

**1** Lay a sheet of brown paper over your work surface. Work the clay into an oval shape. Then knead 1 end of the oval so that it becomes narrower and forms a neck (Fig. 1). The shoulders will be added later.

**Fig. 1**

**2** Using the facial divisions in Fig. 2 as a guide, add facial features in their respective places. Use your modeling tools or your fingers to smooth out the contours.

**3** Take a small piece of clay and build up the chin. This will also help define the jawline (Fig. 3).

**Fig. 3**

*jaw*

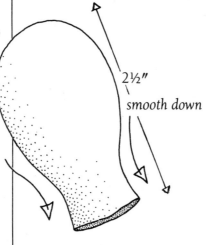

2½″

*smooth down*

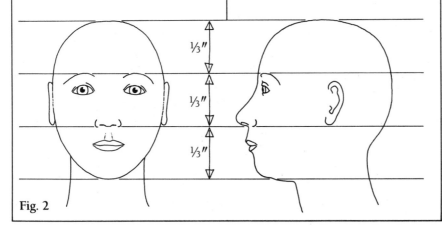

**Fig. 2**

⅓″

⅓″

⅓″

**4** With your thumbs, make slight indentations for the eye positions (Fig. 4).

*indent*

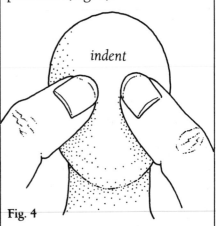

**Fig. 4**

**5** Using your modeling tools, mold a small piece of clay into an elongated triangle shape for the nose and place it in position. Using your fingers, smooth it into the face, and shape to soften (Fig. 5).

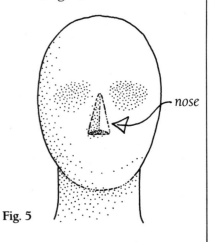

*nose*

**Fig. 5**

**6** Mold another small piece of clay into a flap shape for the upper lip, and place it under the nose. Smooth it in. Mold a smaller roll, and blend this in for the lower lip (Fig. 6).

**Fig. 6**

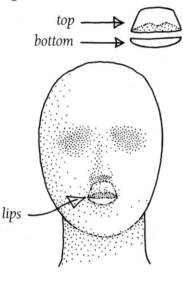

top →
bottom →

lips

**7** Mold another flap shape to fit across the eyebrow line, and smooth it in (Fig. 7).

brow

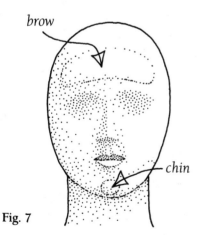

chin

**Fig. 7**

**8** Make a small circle of clay and smooth it onto the face to build up the chin (Fig. 7).

**9** Take the blunt end of a pencil, and push it into each eye to form the sockets (Fig. 8).

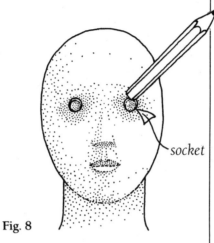

socket

**Fig. 8**

**10** Roll 2 small clay balls and place these into the sockets as eyeballs. Remove some of the clay if the balls are too big, and roll again. When you have the exact size, make sure that the 2 balls match (Fig. 9).

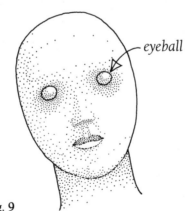

eyeball

**Fig. 9**

**11** To make the eyelids, shape 2 small, flat half-moon strips from the clay for the top eyelids, and 2 others slightly smaller and

flatter. Smooth the larger ones in above each eye, and the smaller ones below (Fig. 10).

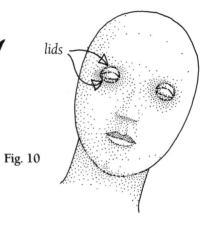

lids

**Fig. 10**

**12** Take the sharp end of your pencil and pierce 2 holes for nostrils at the end of the nose.

**13** For each ear, mold a crescent shape in a size that's appropriate for the head and smooth it into position. Indent each shape with your little finger and add a small clay ball to make an earlobe (Fig. 11).

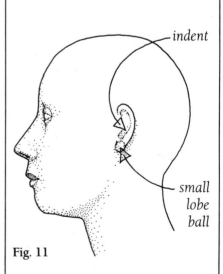

indent

small lobe ball

**Fig. 11**

**14** To create the shoulders, first add small amounts of clay to the neck, then mold it down and out from the neck to form the shoulders and the top of the chest. Flatten it off along the bottom with your knife (Fig. 12A).

**Fig. 12A**

**15** Use the modeling tool to refine the facial details (Fig. 12B).

*refine facial detail*

**16** Lay the head and shoulder piece on a baking sheet and set it aside while you mold the arms and legs.

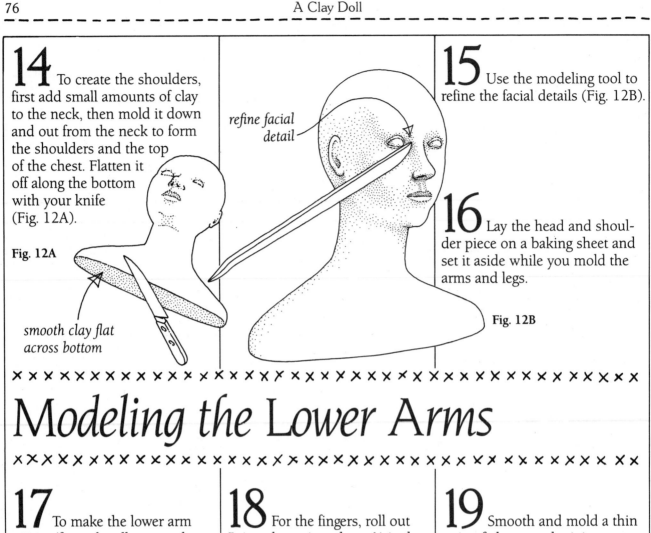

*smooth clay flat across bottom*

**Fig. 12B**

# Modeling the Lower Arms

**17** To make the lower arm pieces (from the elbows to the fingertips), take 2 pieces of clay, equal in size, and roll them into sausage shapes, about 3 inches long. Mold 1 end of each arm into a mitten shape, for the doll's hands (Fig. 13).

**18** For the fingers, roll out 5 tiny clay strips, about ½ inch each. Using your fingers, smooth these onto the mitten end of 1 arm, placing 4 together for the fingers and 1 at the side for the thumb (Fig. 14). Make sure they are well attached on both the front and back of the hand. Trim the finger lengths proportionate to each other, using your own hand as a guide.

**19** Smooth and mold a thin strip of clay over the joins to strengthen them (Fig. 15). Mold the knuckles.

**Fig. 15**

*thin clay strip*

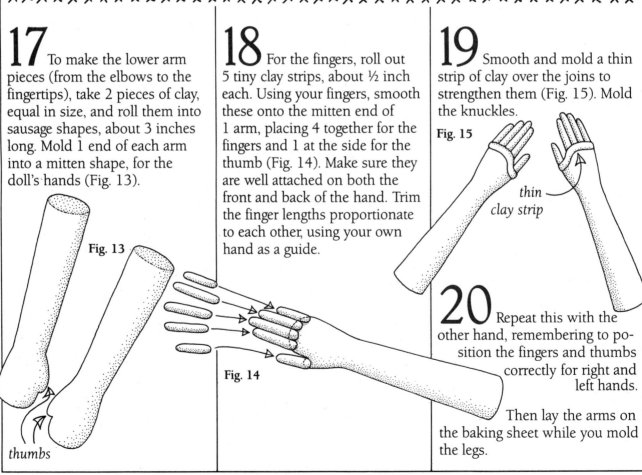

**Fig. 13**

**Fig. 14**

*thumbs*

**20** Repeat this with the other hand, remembering to position the fingers and thumbs correctly for right and left hands.

Then lay the arms on the baking sheet while you mold the legs.

# Modeling the Lower Legs

Before molding the legs, decide what style shoe you want, as this will determine the shape of the doll's feet.

**21** Roll 2 strips of clay into sausage shapes, about 5¾ inches long. Bend them into L shapes, leaving a piece 3½ inches long for the distance from calf to ankle. The foot should measure 2¼ inches from heel to toe (Fig. 16).

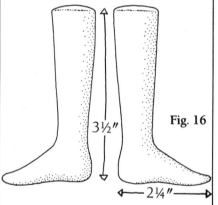

3½"

**Fig. 16**

←— 2¼" —→

**22** Use a modeling tool to shape the shoe area. Add small strips or circles of clay for straps, buttons, or other shoe designs (Fig. 17).

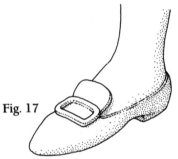

**Fig. 17**

**23** When they are complete, lay the legs on the baking sheet with the other pieces. Bake in a preheated oven at the temperature indicated on the clay packaging (usually 250°F) for about 10 minutes (Fig. 18).

**24** When the clay is baked, allow it to cool. The pieces are now ready to be painted.

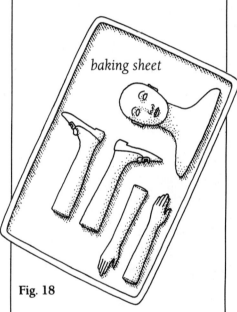

baking sheet

**Fig. 18**

# Painting the Clay

When using acrylic paints, work quickly and evenly as they dry fast. Test the shades you mix on white scrap paper first. .

**25** Begin by mixing up a skin tone. When you have a color you like, paint it smoothly over the head piece with the medium-size brush (Fig. 19).

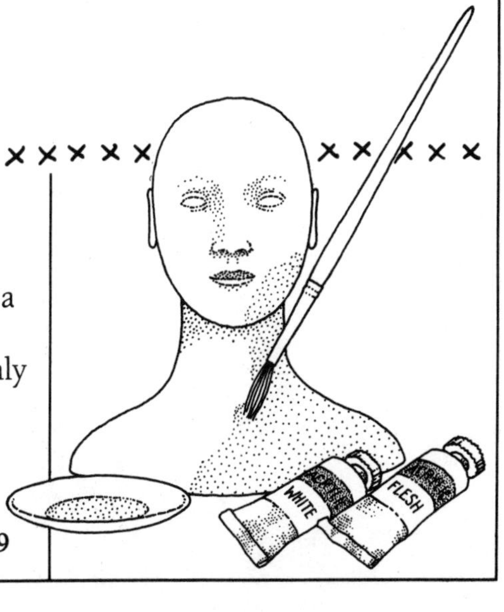

**Fig. 19**

**26** Before the paint dries, dab a spot of red or orange onto the cheek area with the fine brush. It should blend into the skin tone rather than dry on the surface (Fig. 20).

**Fig. 20**

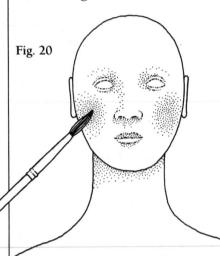

**27** Mix a light color for the eyes—blue, brown, or green, with white—and paint a circle for the iris in the center of the eyeball (Fig. 21).

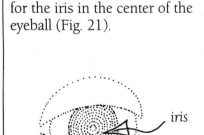

*iris*

**Fig. 21**

**28** Using a light brown wash, paint the upper eyelid, and line the lower lid. Shade the outer edges above to make them darker (Fig. 22).

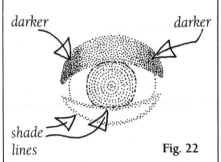

*darker*          *darker*

*shade lines*                **Fig. 22**

**29** Define all around the iris with a darker shade of brown. Add a small black circle to make the pupil, and line the eyelid top and bottom (Fig. 23). Then add a tiny dot of white to the center of the pupil.

**Fig. 23**

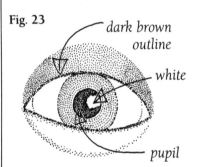

*dark brown outline*

*white*

*pupil*

**30** Sketch in the eyebrows with a pencil, then paint over the pencil lines using a light brown paint (Fig. 24).

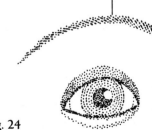

**Fig. 24**

**31** For the lips, mix a pale orange-pink or use red. Color in the lips and when dry, outline the shape with a fine line in brown or red around and between the lips (Fig. 25).

**Fig. 25**

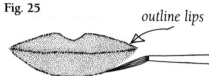

*outline lips*

**32** Paint the hands and lower arms in flesh tone.

**33** For the legs, paint on shoes and stockings in colors you like (Fig. 26).

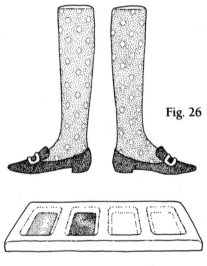

**Fig. 26**

# Making the Cloth Body

×××××××××××××××××××××××××××××××××××××××××××××

**34** Measure the circumference around the clay shoulders (here it is approximately 8 inches). Halve this. Lay a good-size piece of brown wrapping paper on a table, and draw a line of this length (4 inches) onto it (Fig. 27). Draw a torso shape in proportion, using the full drawing in Step 35 (Fig. 28) as a guide. From shoulder to hip line should measure 5 inches.

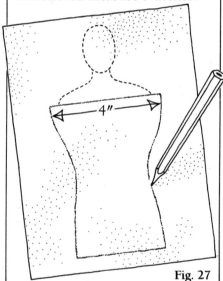

**Fig. 27**

**35** A guide for body measurements:

Shoulder to elbow: 3 inches
Elbow to fingertips: 3½ inches
Hip to knee: 3½ inches
Knee to toes: 5¾ inches

The wrist should be in line with the hip, and the elbow in line with the waist. From the hips through the feet should equal the distance from the top of the head to the hips.

**Fig. 28**

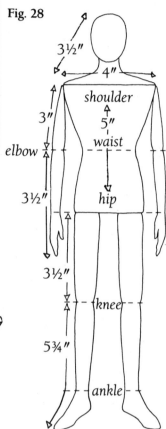

3½"
4"
*shoulder*
3"
5"
*waist*
*elbow*
*hip*
3½"
3½"
*knee*
5¾"
*ankle*

**36** Find the center point on both the shoulder and hip lines, and draw a vertical line from one to the other. Fold the paper along this line, and cut out the torso shape (Fig. 29).

**Fig. 29**

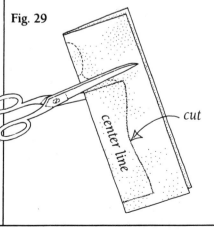

*center line*

*cut*

**37** Take the unbleached muslin, lay it flat, then fold it in half evenly. Pin the open paper pattern to it, and allowing 1 inch all around for seams, cut it out (Fig. 30). Remove the paper pattern, and pin and stitch the side and bottom seams only.

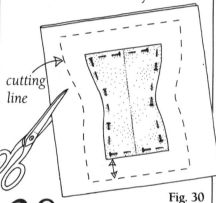

*cutting line*

**Fig. 30**

**38** Measure the circumference of the top of a clay leg. Cut out 2 pieces of muslin ½ inch wider than this, and the same length as the clay leg. These will be the upper legs. Glue one end of one of the pieces neatly around the top of a clay leg. Let this dry (Fig. 31).

**Fig. 31**

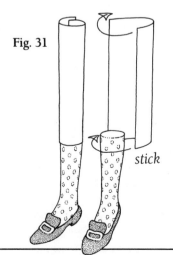

*stick*

**39** Pin up the side seam and sew with an overcast stitch, leaving the top open.

**40** Stuff some Kapok well down into the leg with a pencil. When you have reached knee height, leave an unstuffed gap of about 1 inch. Pin across this gap and stitch it closed (Fig. 32).

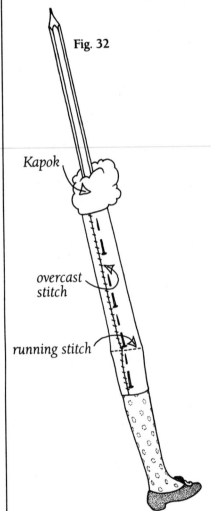

**Fig. 32**

*Kapok*

*overcast stitch*

*running stitch*

**41** Continue stuffing until you are near the top. Again, pin across and close with a running stitch. Fold in the top seams, and pin the leg into position on

the body shape. Stitch it on with an overcast stitch. Do the same for the other leg (Fig. 33).

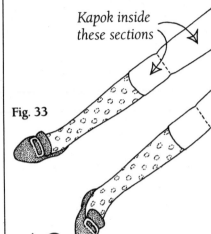

*Kapok inside these sections*

**Fig. 33**

**42** Repeat the same procedure for the arms. Pin and stitch at the elbow joint and just below the shoulder joint. Fold down the top seams and sew the arms to the shoulder area using an overcast stitch. Check that you have the hands on the correct sides before you sew them on (Fig. 34).

**Fig. 34**

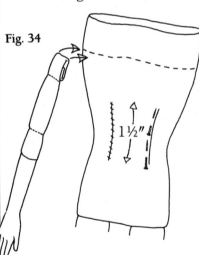

1½"

**43** To shape the torso, hemstitch darts into the front and back (Fig. 34). Make the front darts deeper than the back darts to define a breast area.

**44** Turn the torso shape right side out, and fill it solidly with Kapok.

**45** Fold in the 1-inch seam allowance at the top of the torso, and attach this to the clay shoulder base using white glue (Fig. 35).

**Fig. 35**

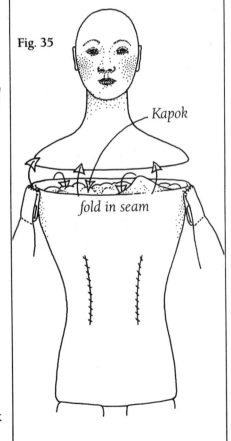

*Kapok*

*fold in seam*

# Attaching the Hair

The easiest way to give your doll hair is to find a wig the proper size and glue it on. But wigs can be hard to find in the size you need, and they often look bulky on the doll's head. I prefer to glue the hair on in layers. This method is time-consuming, but the results are worth it.

Human hair is heavy to work with, especially on a smaller doll. Mohair looks the best and is the easiest to work with, but it may be hard to find. You can also use yarn or silk embroidery thread. White glue is the best adhesive for all of these choices.

Choose a hairstyle before you begin. Determine if there will be a part, where the part will be, and how the hairline should lie. My doll has a center part with the hair covering her ears.

**46** To begin, take a small bunch of mohair (or whatever hair material you are using), and holding it in your fingers, cut a straight edge across the top (Fig. 36).

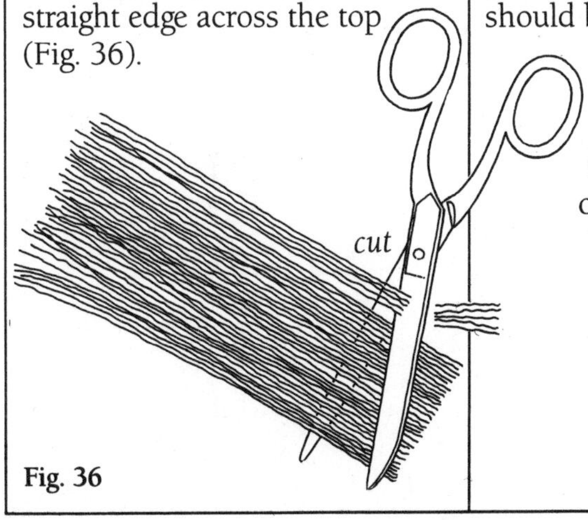

*cut*

**Fig. 36**

**47** Smear a line of white glue along the straight edge of the mohair, and also a thin line across the base at the back of the head. Align the mohair along the glue line on the back of the head and press it into place with a pin (Fig. 37). Let this dry for 3 to 5 minutes.

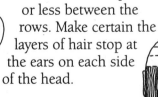

**Fig. 37**

**48** Continue doing this with more rows of hair, up to the spot where the back of the part would come (Fig. 38). There should be about ½-inch space or less between the rows. Make certain the layers of hair stop at the ears on each side of the head.

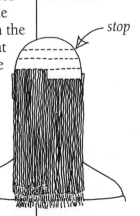

**Fig. 38**

**49** Lightly pencil in a hairline on both sides of the head (Fig. 39).

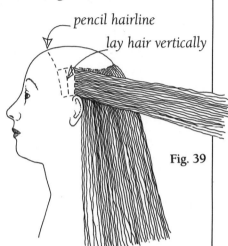

*pencil hairline*
*lay hair vertically*

**Fig. 39**

**50** Starting from the hairline, draw three ½-inch-long vertical lines up from 1 ear. The last one should meet the attached hair (Fig. 39). These lines will be your guide for gluing on the hair in vertical rows above the ear. Working forward, attach the hair in rows above the ear, following the vertical lines. Repeat this on the other side of the head.

*stop*

**51** Draw a line from the center of the forehead, on the hairline, down to the top of the attached hair at the back of the head. This line will be your guide for the center part. Draw 3 horizontal lines on each side of the center part. These lines will serve as a guide for attaching the hair to the top of the head. Start at the lowest line on 1 side of the head and attach the hair in rows until you reach the center part. As you reach the top of the head, decrease the amount of hair (Fig. 40). Repeat this on the other side of the head.

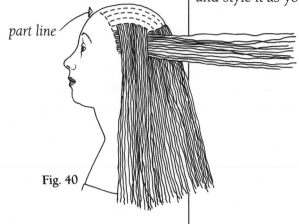

part line

Fig. 40

**52** Let the hair dry for 1 hour, then gently comb, trim, and style it as you like.

# Making the Dress

When making clothes for a doll, I always work directly from the doll. Since this one has a cloth body, it is easy to pin materials to her. Try out different colors of fabrics and trim before making a final selection.

**53** To make the bodice, lay the doll flat and measure the distance from shoulder to shoulder and the length from neck to waist. My doll is 4 inches from shoulder to shoulder and 3 inches from neck to waist (Fig. 41).

**54** For the bodice front, cut a piece of fabric 5 inches wide and 4 inches long. For the bodice back, cut another piece of fabric 6 inches wide and 4 inches long. Fold the fabric for the back in half across the width and cut it into two 3-inch pieces.

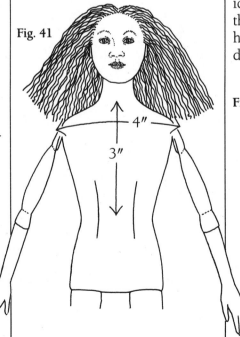

Fig. 41

4"

3"

**55** Pin the bodice front fabric to the front of the doll, wrong side out. Pin a ½-inch hem on each of the 2 back bodice pieces. Pin these 2 pieces to the back of the doll so that the hems meet at the center of the doll's back (Fig. 42).

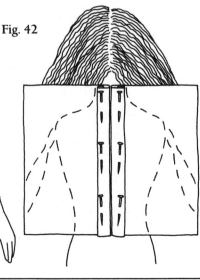

Fig. 42

**56** Pin the fabric together along the shoulder line. Following this line, trim away the excess fabric, leaving ¼-inch seam allowance. Snip the fabric down the center of the neck area (Fig. 43).

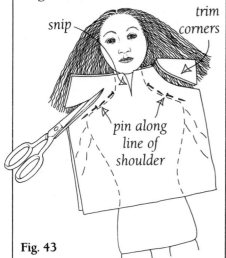

**Fig. 43**

**57** Pin the side seams at the waist and snip. Pin the side seams from under the arms to just below the waist. Trim away the excess fabric, leaving ¼-inch seam allowance. Snip the seam allowance (Fig. 44).

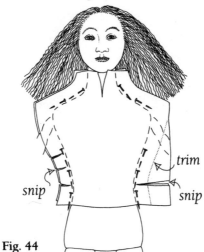

**Fig. 44**

**58** Mark the neck and waist lines on the front and back of the dress bodice with a pencil. Dropping them a little below their actual positions, mark the armholes as well.

**59** Remove the bodice from the doll. Stitch together the side and shoulder seams. Leaving the back open, stitch down the center hems. Trim away the extra neck material, and finish the neckline with facing if you wish (see Dressed Rag Doll, Steps 49–51). Press the seams open. Turn the bodice right side out, and place it on the doll.

# Making the Skirt

**60** Measure from the waist to the length you have chosen—just below the knee, or at the calf or ankle. Cut a 36-inch-wide piece of fabric to that length plus 1½ inches (Fig. 45). For my doll, the length of the fabric is 11½ inches.

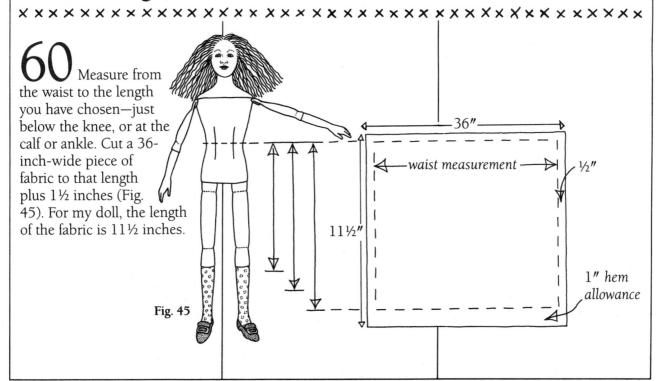

**Fig. 45**

**61** Fold the fabric piece in half, wrong side out, and pin the open ends together, leaving a ½-inch seam allowance. Sew the seam up with running stitches to 1 inch below the top. Press this seam flat. Turn up and sew a 1-inch hem around the bottom (Fig. 46).

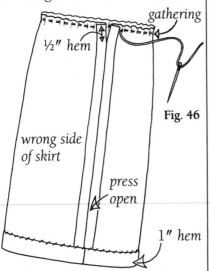

*gathering*

½″ *hem*

*wrong side of skirt*

*press open*

1″ *hem*

**Fig. 46**

**62** Make a gathering stitch ¼ inch down around the top of the fabric, and gather it loosely, leaving the final gathering until the next stage (Fig. 46).

**63** Pull the skirt upside down over the doll's head, until the gathering line meets the bottom of the bodice. Match up the back seams and pin the skirt and bodice together, pulling the gathering thread as necessary. Tie off (Fig. 47).

**64** Remove the dress from the doll and stitch the skirt to the bodice with a running stitch. Snip and trim the seam allowance to ⅜ inch.

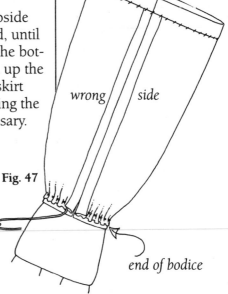

*wrong* / *side*

**Fig. 47**

*pull in*

*end of bodice*

× × × × × × × × × × × × × × × × × × × × × × × × × × × × × × × × × × × × × ×

# Adding the Sleeves

× × × × × × × × × × × × × × × × × × × × × × × × × × × × × × × × × × × × × ×

**65** Cut out 2 rectangles of fabric—for my doll, the pieces are 5½ inches long by 4½ inches wide. Fold each in half lengthways and pin wrong side out. Measure the width of the armhole on the bodice. Allowing extra material for seams, pencil a diagonal line from the top of the fold to the open side. The line should be the length of the armhole. From this point, and again allowing extra for seams, draw another diagonal down to the cuff line. Trim away the fabric at these lines (Fig. 48).

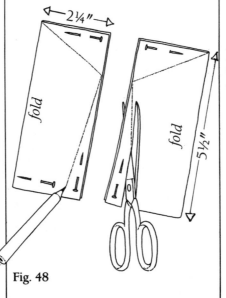

←—2¼″—→

*fold*

*fold*

5½″

**Fig. 48**

**66** Open out the fabric pieces, and round off the top center point with scissors (Fig. 49).

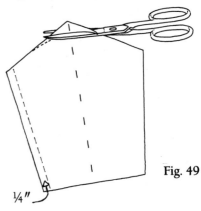

¼″

**Fig. 49**

**67** Pin up a hem for each cuff, and pin the side seams together. Sew these up with a running stitch (Fig. 50).

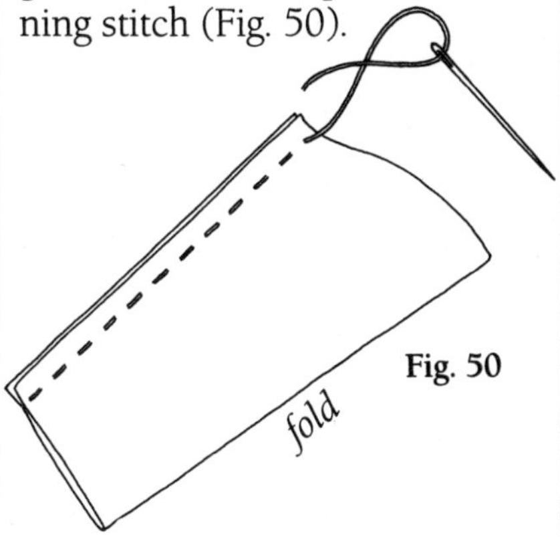

*fold*  **Fig. 50**

**68** With sleeves inside out, sew a gathering stitch along the rounded cap, and gather loosely. Turn the sleeves and dress right side out. Set each sleeve into an armhole. Adjust the gathering and pin (Fig. 51). Turn the dress inside out once again and sew the sleeves in place.

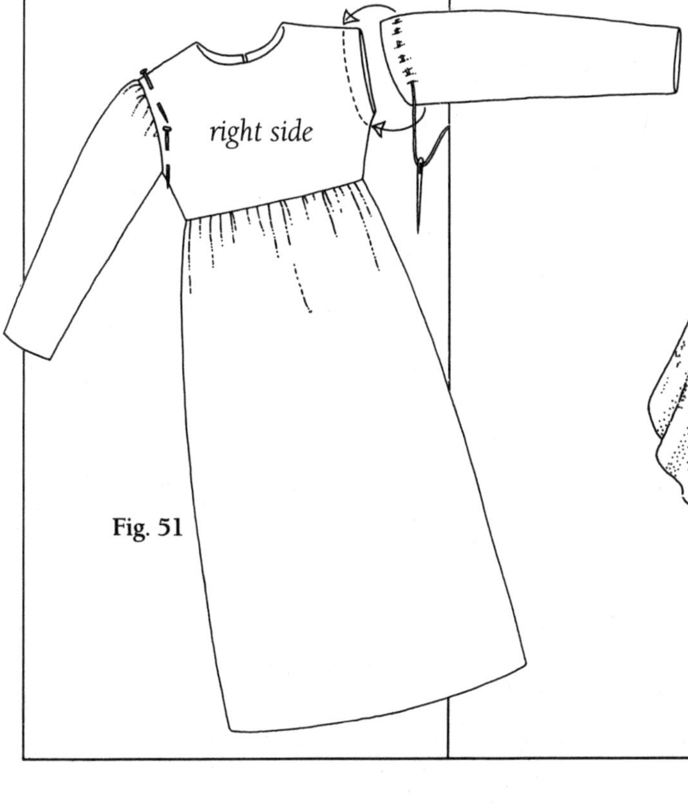

*right side*

**Fig. 51**

**69** To join the back of the dress, sew on two or three small buttons and make eye loops with embroidery thread to correspond (Fig. 52).

**Fig. 52**

**70** Now you have the basic dress for your doll. Make additions as you like from your scrap bag—add lace for the collar and cuffs, a petticoat, trims, and accessories.

# A Wax Doll

**A**lthough wax dolls take more time to make than other dolls do, the result is worth the effort. Wax gives the "skin" of a doll a translucent quality that is very realistic. The key to success in making a wax doll is patience. Once mastered, it is a rewarding technique.

## You Will Need

Plasticine
Kitchen knife
Tape measure and ruler
Modeling tools (available from art supply stores): 6-inch wire-end modeling tool, 6-inch wood modeling tool
Pencil
Old towel
Rolling pin
Pins
1 pound plaster of paris
Wooden sticks for stirring
Old kitchen spoon
Old paintbrushes
Dishwashing liquid
Bucket
Paper towels
Kitchen string
Measuring cups
Paraffin

Beeswax
Old saucepan or coffee can
Pot holders
Oil paint (flesh-tone, white, brown, red, orange-red)
Aluminum foil
Paintbrushes (fine)
Paper clip
Brown wrapping paper
1 yard unbleached muslin
Scissors
Needle and thread (an assortment)
Kapok
Turpentine
Felt-tip pen
Light cotton net or gauze
White glue
Hair (mohair, crepe, or wool yarn, or an old wig)
Lace for petticoat, 28 inches long and 7 inches wide

Steam iron
Cotton fabric scrap
Snaps
1 yard cotton fabric for dress
6 small buttons
1 yard cotton fabric for pinafore
Cotton fabric for bloomers, 24 inches long and 10 inches wide
Small piece of stretch fabric for stockings
Small piece of thin suede or other heavy fabric for shoes
Small piece of oaktag
Masking tape
Small piece of dark brown leather or felt
Old straw hat
Elastic string
Darning needle

# Making the Plaster Casts

×  ×  ×  ×  ×  ×  ×  ×  ×  ×  ×  ×  ×  ×  ×  ×  ×  ×  ×  ×  ×  ×  ×  ×  ×  ×  ×  ×  ×  ×  ×  ×  ×  ×  ×  ×  ×  ×  ×

When making the model for your plaster cast, be on the lookout for awkward recesses or angles, called undercuts, which will prevent the plaster mold from releasing the wax easily. These deep recesses often occur between the chin and neck and in the nose and cheek area. If this happens, you will probably have to break the mold in order to remove the wax head, and may damage the head in the process. It is much better to see where you have made the undercut and begin again from scratch. Ideally you will be able to remove the model head without difficulty the first time. Go slowly.

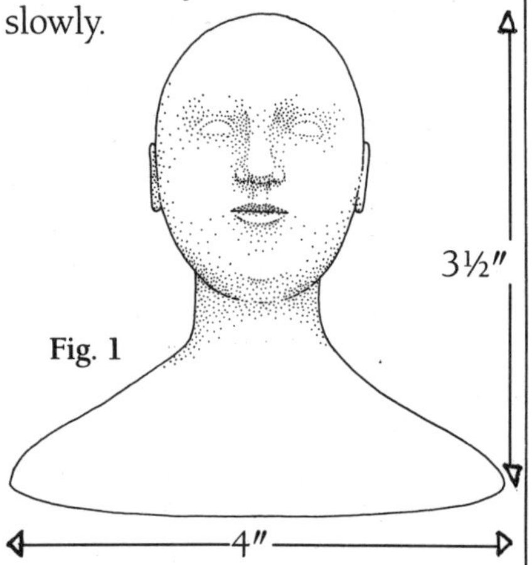

**Fig. 1**

3½″

4″

**1** Following Steps 1–15 for the clay doll, use Plasticine to mold a head and shoulders. The size is up to you, but I prefer to keep mine fairly small. The wax doll is proportionately the same as the clay one—3½ inches from the top of the head to the bottom of the shoulders; 4 inches wide from shoulder to shoulder (Fig. 1).

**2** When the model is ready, lay it flat on an old towel. Roll out a strip of Plasticine ¼ inch thick. The length should be the distance from shoulder to shoulder, over the head (Fig. 2).

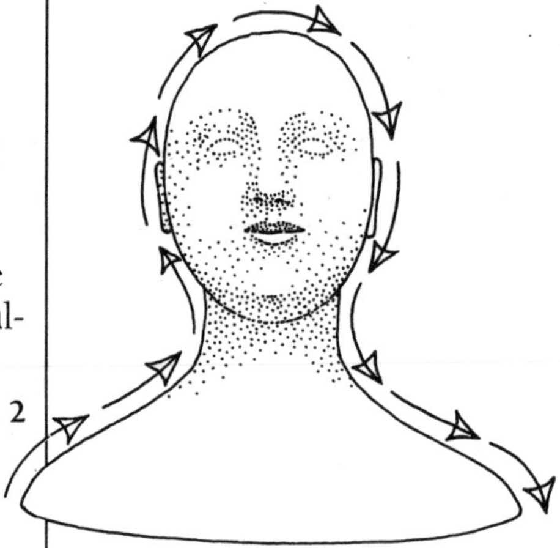

**Fig. 2**

*measure*

**3** Cut a 2-inch-wide strip from the Plasticine and lay this around the head and shoulders. Press it gently to the head to help it stay in place. It should divide the front and back of the model evenly (Figs. 3A, 3B). It may help to score a pin line over the center profile of the model and match the strip to this.

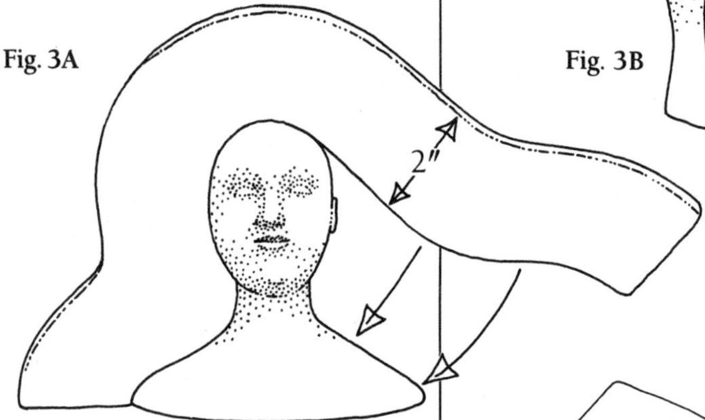

**Fig. 3A**

2″

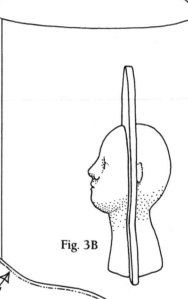

**Fig. 3B**

**4** Mix up the plaster of paris following package directions. As it starts to set, spoon it over the face, up to the edge of the Plasticine strip (Fig. 4). Let it set for about 15 minutes.

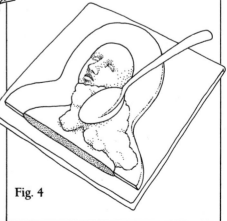

**Fig. 4**

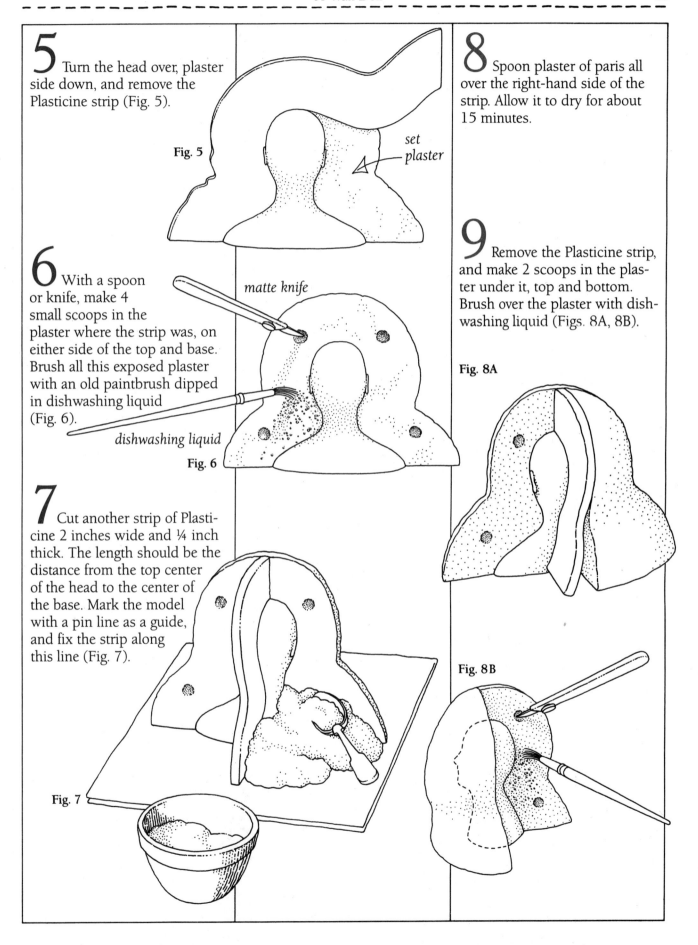

**5** Turn the head over, plaster side down, and remove the Plasticine strip (Fig. 5).

**Fig. 5**

*set plaster*

**6** With a spoon or knife, make 4 small scoops in the plaster where the strip was, on either side of the top and base. Brush all this exposed plaster with an old paintbrush dipped in dishwashing liquid (Fig. 6).

*matte knife*

*dishwashing liquid*

**Fig. 6**

**7** Cut another strip of Plasticine 2 inches wide and ¼ inch thick. The length should be the distance from the top center of the head to the center of the base. Mark the model with a pin line as a guide, and fix the strip along this line (Fig. 7).

**Fig. 7**

**8** Spoon plaster of paris all over the right-hand side of the strip. Allow it to dry for about 15 minutes.

**9** Remove the Plasticine strip, and make 2 scoops in the plaster under it, top and bottom. Brush over the plaster with dishwashing liquid (Figs. 8A, 8B).

**Fig. 8A**

**Fig. 8B**

**10** Spoon plaster of paris over the remaining section and allow it to dry for about 15 minutes. Turn the model upside down, and scrape the base smooth with a knife (Fig. 9).

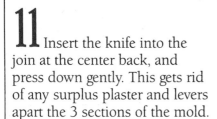

**Fig. 9**

**11** Insert the knife into the join at the center back, and press down gently. This gets rid of any surplus plaster and levers apart the 3 sections of the mold.

If necessary, do the same with the overhead join (Figs. 10A, 10B, 10C).

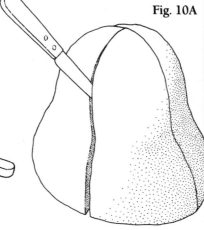

**Fig. 10A**

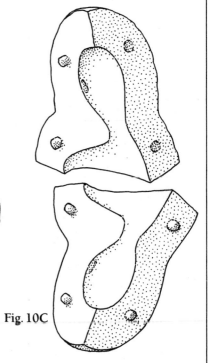

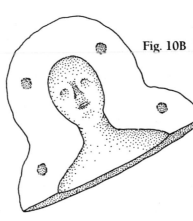

**Fig. 10B**   **Fig. 10C**

**12** Your Plasticine model should now slip out easily.

# Modeling the Arms and Legs

**13** Following Steps 17–19 for the clay doll, make a pair of arms and hands. Make sure that the fingers are all touching; otherwise they are liable to break off. For a 3½-inch head, the diameter of the arm is ½ to ⅝ inch (Fig. 11).

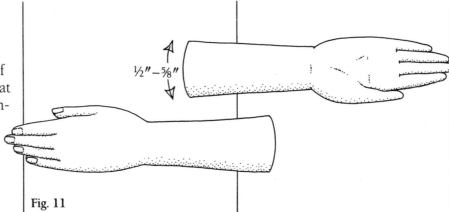

½″–⅝″

**Fig. 11**

**14** Roll out a strip of Plasticine ¼ inch thick. Cut a piece 2 inches wide and twice the length of the arm and hand. Mold and lay the strip around the arm and hand, but not across the elbow end (Fig. 12).

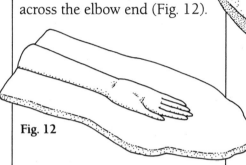

**Fig. 12**

**15** Cover one side with plaster of paris, and allow it to set for 15 minutes.

**16** Turn the arm over and remove the Plasticine strip. Scoop out 4 holes—2 on opposite sides at each end. Coat all

this area of plaster with dish-washing liquid (Fig. 13).

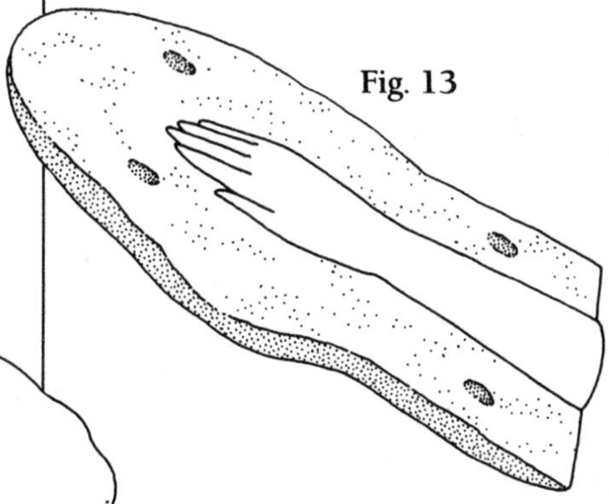

**Fig. 13**

**17** Cover the second side with plaster, and allow it to dry for 15 minutes. Then pry the 2 sections apart with a knife.

**18** Repeat the whole procedure for the other arm and hand.

**19** To make the legs, follow the instructions in Steps 21–22 for the clay doll. Make sure that you choose a basic shoe shape. (Instructions for removable shoes appear on page 104.) Then follow the procedure for making the molds, as you did for the arms (Fig. 14).

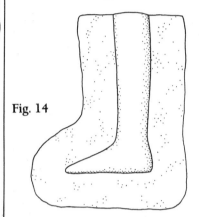

**Fig. 14**

**20** You should now have 11 sections of molding. Let these soak overnight in a bucket of water.

# Pouring the Wax

**21** Take the molds out of the water, and let the surfaces dry only for about 10 minutes. (The inner plaster needs to remain wet in order to release the wax easily.) You can help remove some of the excess water by using paper towels.

**22** Coat the insides of the molds with dishwashing liquid. Place the 3 head sections together and lay strips of Plasticine over the outer join lines. This helps to make a full seal. Tie the form together with string (Fig. 15).

*Plasticine strips*

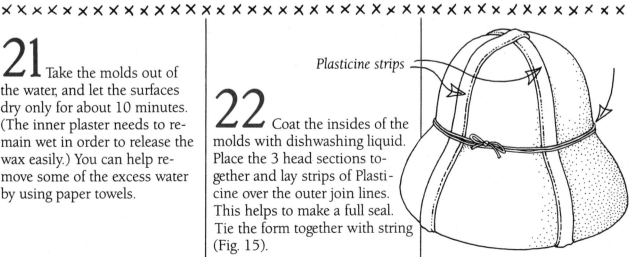

**Fig. 15**

**23** Mix 2 cups paraffin to 1 cup beeswax in a pot you no longer use for cooking or in an empty coffee can. Turn a stove burner on very low and put the container on it (Fig. 16). Remember, *this mixture is highly inflammable.* For extra safety, you can place the container in a pan of water and then heat the water. (Use pot holders when handling the wax pot.) When the mixture is runny, gradually add drops of flesh-colored oil paint, stirring constantly with a wooden stick.

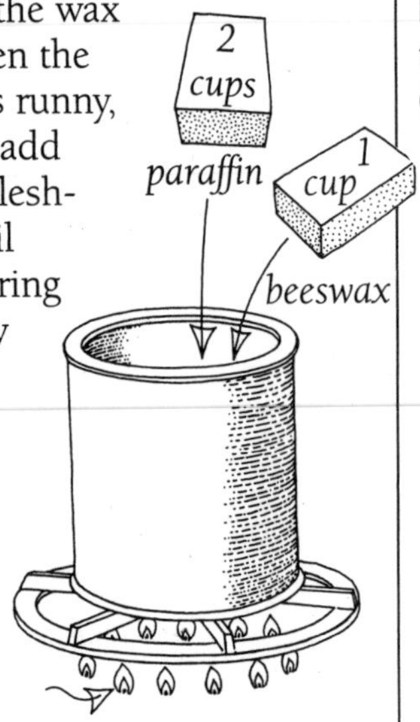

*2 cups*

*paraffin*   *1 cup*

*beeswax*

**Fig. 16**

**24** Pour a little wax onto a piece of aluminum foil to test the color. It dries quickly, so you can soon see the result (Fig. 17).

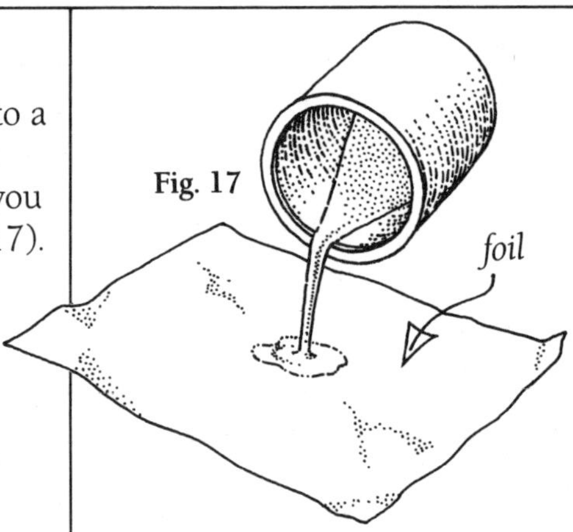

When you have a good color, turn the plaster mold upside down, wedging it between books. Pour the melted wax into the mold right up to the top (Fig. 18).

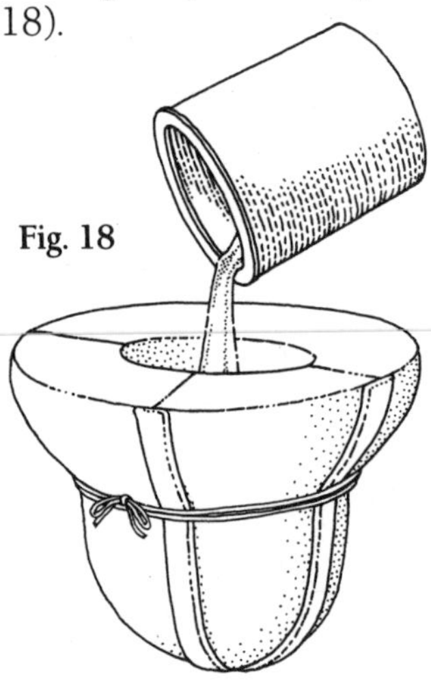

**Fig. 18**

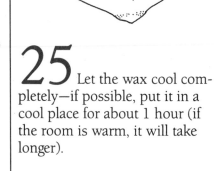

**Fig. 17**

*foil*

**25** Let the wax cool completely—if possible, put it in a cool place for about 1 hour (if the room is warm, it will take longer).

**26** Follow the same procedure for each arm and leg: Lay a Plasticine strip over the join, and tie the pieces together. Pour in the wax and let it set. Put the arms and legs in a cool place to set thoroughly.

x x x x x x x x x x x x x x x x x x x x x x x x x x x x x x x x x x x x x x x x x x x x x x x x

# Breaking the Molds

x x x x x x x x x x x x x x x x x x x x x x x x x x x x x x x x x x x x x x x x x x x x x x x x

**27** After an hour, check to see if the wax in the head and shoulders mold is firm. If it is, untie the strings and remove the Plasticine strips. Carefully ease the seams apart with a knife. Start with the center back seam on the head, and remove the 2 back sections first. Then take hold of the wax model and jiggle it very gently to loosen it from the plaster. If the wax model should break, don't panic. Place the pieces to one side and continue removing the remaining pieces from the molds. Broken pieces can be rejoined with the help of hot melted wax. Use the wax the same way you would use glue to mend broken china. Once the broken piece is attached securely, smooth over small cracks, holes, and nicks by painting on additional hot wax with a small brush. Smooth it further with a modeling tool (Fig. 19).

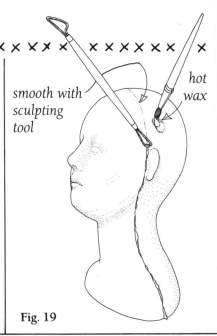

*smooth with sculpting tool*

*hot wax*

**Fig. 19**

**28** Separate the arm and leg molds and remove the wax limbs.

**29** Smooth away any seams or ridges with a knife or modeling tool. Also smooth out any bubbles. If necessary, define the mouth, nose, eyes, fingers, shoes, etc.

**30** Using your modeling tool or a knife, gently hollow out the shoulder area of the head piece. Leave the shoulder walls ⅜ inch thick. Hollow out the elbow and knee ends of each arm and leg about ⅝ inch deep. The wax walls should be ⅛ inch thick.

**31** With a tool made from a bent paper clip (Fig. 20A), scoop out 4 holes from the shoulder walls, 2 in the front and 2 in the back, ½ inch in from each end (Fig. 20B). Also scoop out 2 holes ½ inch down from the top of the arm pieces, and 4 holes ½ inch down from the top of the legs (Fig. 21).

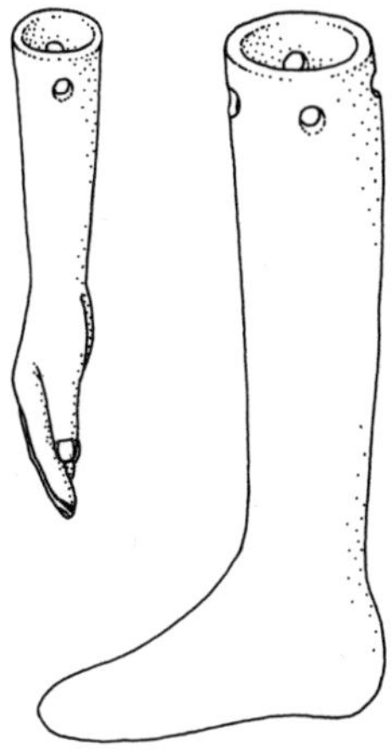

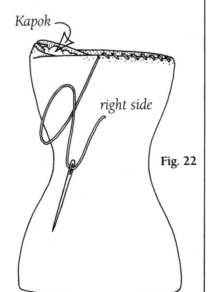

**Fig. 21**

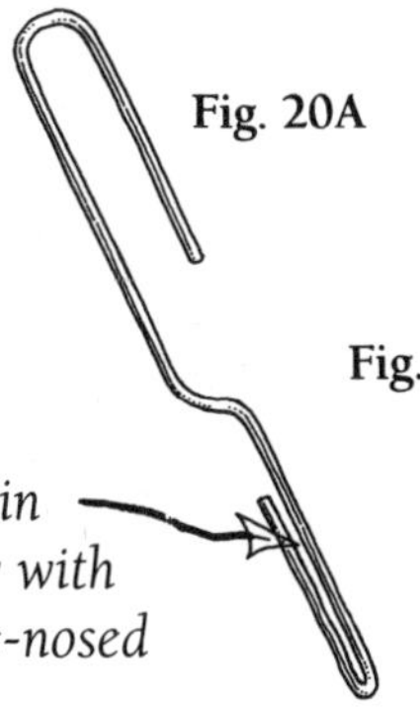

**Fig. 20A**

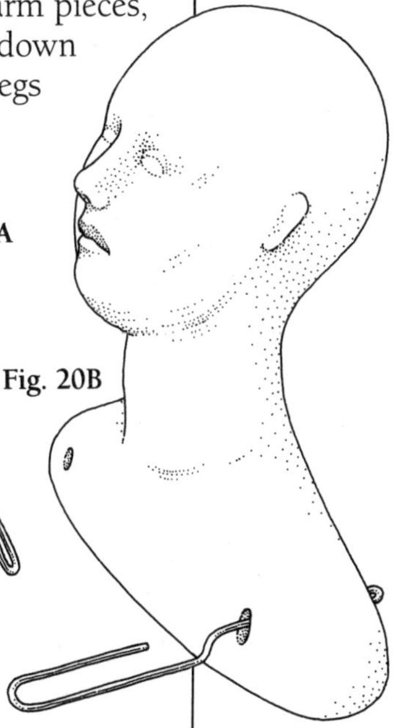

**Fig. 20B**

*pinch in tightly with needle-nosed pliers*

# Making the Cloth Body

**32** Following Steps 34–37 for the clay doll, cut out a muslin body shape. Turn under 1 inch on each of the side seams and the top seam and stitch closed. Snip the seam allowance around this, then turn it right side out.

*Kapok*

*right side*

**Fig. 22**

**33** Fill the body shape from top to bottom with Kapok. When it is firmly packed, fold in the bottom seam allowance about ½ inch, pin together, and stitch closed with small overcast stitches (Fig. 22). Make darts following Step 43 of the clay doll.

**34** Cut out 2 pieces of muslin that measure the length of the wax arms and the width of their circumference. Allow an extra ½ inch for seams. Pin and stitch the bottom and side seams. Snip the seam allowance. Turn right side out (Fig. 23).

**Fig. 23**

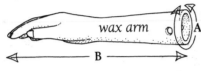

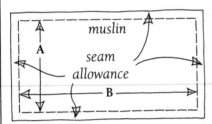

**35** Stuff each arm with Kapok to within 1 inch of the top. Close the stuffing off at this point with a running stitch. Then fold in the top edges ½ inch and sew them together (Fig. 24).

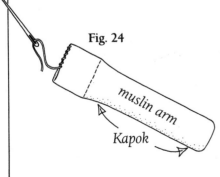

**36** Cut out 2 pieces of muslin the length and circumference of the legs, and follow the same sewing and stuffing method as for the arms.

**37** Press the top of the cloth body into the hollow of the wax shoulders base (Fig. 25A). Stitch through the holes to attach. Starting at the back, loop thread from the torso over and through the hole in the right shoulder, then through the body and out and over the hole in the front of the body (Fig. 25B). Do this several times to secure the right side. Repeat for the other shoulder (Fig. 25C).

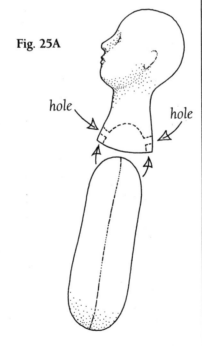

Fig. 25A

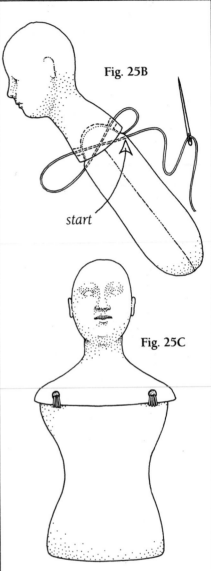

Fig. 25B

Fig. 25C

**38** Press the bottom (stuffed) end of each cloth leg into the hollow top of the wax leg section. Stitch the 2 pieces together securely through the carved holes in the wax (Fig. 26).

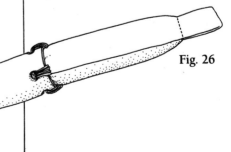

Fig. 26

**39** Follow the same procedure for the arms.

**40** Pin, then using an overcast stitch, sew the cloth legs and arms to the body (Fig. 27).

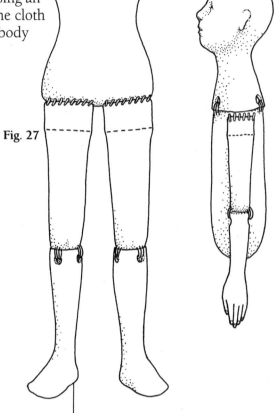

**Fig. 27**

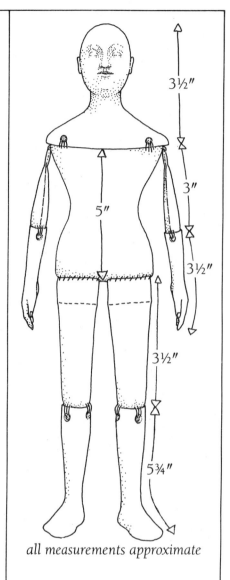

3½"

3"

5"

3½"

3½"

3½"

5¾"

*all measurements approximate*

# Painting the Features

Because the wax is already tinted with a flesh tone, you only have to highlight some areas and paint in the features.

**41** Start with a little flesh-colored oil paint mixed with white. Apply the paint with a fine brush above the eyes and down the center of the nose. Dab the color in with your finger. This blends the color smoothly into the face. Use a mixture of orange and red for the lips and cheeks, dabbing the cheek color on with your finger. Paint in the eyes, saving the darkest color (brown, not black) for the finest details on the pupils. (Use the brown to highlight the nostrils, also.) If necessary, thin the colors with turpentine. Try to leave as much of the skin unpainted as possible to bring out the translucent quality of the wax.

# Attaching the Hair

× × × × × × × × × × × × × × × × × × × × × × × × × × × × × × × × × × × × × × × × × × ×

**42** Using a felt-tip pen, mark small dots on the head to indicate the hairline (Fig. 28).

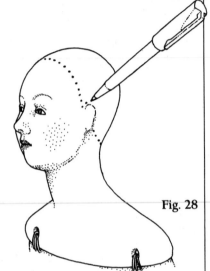

Fig. 28

**43** Cut ½-inch-wide strips of light cotton net or gauze. Place 1 strip along the marked hairline. Indicate the location of the ears with light pencil marks, and cut away the fabric (Fig. 29).

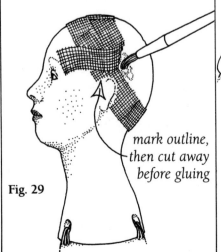

*mark outline, then cut away before gluing*

Fig. 29

**44** Attach the strip to the head with glue or melted wax, using a paintbrush to dab on the wax. Continue until you have smoothly covered the entire back of the head with fabric strips.

**45** Cut a section of mohair straight across the top, and wide enough to extend along the hairline at the back from ear to ear. Apply a thin strip of glue along the top of the hair section and press it firmly to the head (Fig. 30).

*press along base of hairline*

Fig. 30

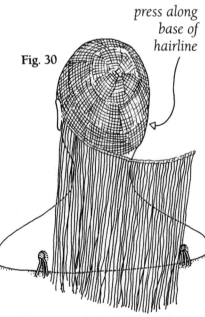

**46** Work upward in layers over the net cap until you reach the midline, pressing each glued section down firmly. Then work

backward from the front of the forehead, starting at the hairline (Fig. 31).

Fig. 31

**47** Let the hair dry for at least 1 hour. Then, brush all the hair forward over the face, and comb it back to style it. Trim the ends if necessary (Fig. 32).

Fig. 32

# Making the Petticoat

×××××××××××××××××××××××××××××××××××××××××××××

I have dressed my doll in a long dress, complete with separate pinafore. Her accessories include hat, shoes, stockings, bloomers, and petticoat.

**48** To make the petticoat, you will need a piece of cotton lace. For the doll shown, that piece is 28 inches long and 7 inches wide. If you don't have a wide enough piece, sew a strip of lace to a piece of white cotton fabric. Fold the strip in half and pin the ends together (Fig. 33).

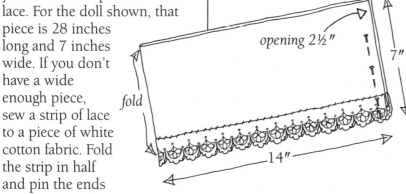

**Fig. 33**

**49** Sew the end seam closed with a running stitch, leaving a 2½-inch opening at the waist edge (if you attached lace to cotton, the cotton is the top of the petticoat). Press the seam open, and tack it down with a basting stitch.

**50** Run a gathering stitch about ½ inch down from the top of the fabric. Put the petticoat on the doll, and tighten the gathers to fit comfortably around the doll's waist. Anchor the thread.

**51** To make the waistband, measure the doll's waist circumference, add 1 inch, and cut a strip of cotton that length and 1 inch wide.

**52** Starting at the waist opening at the back of the petticoat, pin the waistband just below the gathering stitches, right sides facing. Leave a ¾-inch tab on the right and a ¼-inch overlap on the left (Fig. 34).

**Fig. 34**

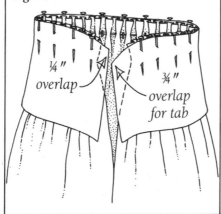

¼" overlap

¾" overlap for tab

**53** Attach the waistband to the petticoat, using a running stitch. Turn the waistband over the top of the gathering to the inside. Turn in a narrow hem and using an overcast stitch, sew the waistband down along the row of stitches showing through the front (Fig. 35).

**Fig. 35**

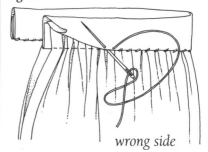

*wrong side*

**54** Turn in the end of the waistband and the edge of the tab and stitch them closed (Fig. 36). Sew on a snap to hold the petticoat closed.

**Fig. 36**

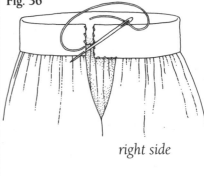

*right side*

# Making the Dress

× × × × × × × × × × × × × × × × × × × × × × × × × × × × × × × × × × × × × × × × × × ×

**55** The dress for the wax doll is similar in style to the dress designed for the clay doll. Follow Steps 53–64 to make this doll's dress.

**56** The sleeves have a different shape, however. To make the sleeve pattern, take a piece of brown paper 5 inches long and 4½ inches wide. Fold it in half so that it measures 4½ by 2½ inches, and draw the outline of the sleeve as shown (Fig. 37). Cut out the pattern.

**Fig. 37**

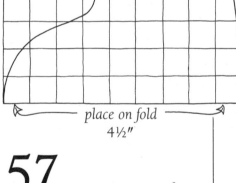

2½″

place on fold
4½″

**57** Cut out 2 pieces of dress fabric 6 inches long and 5½ inches wide. Place the wrong sides of the fabric pieces together. Open out the sleeve pattern and pin it to the fabric pieces. Make sure the center fold lies straight along the grain of the fabric (Fig. 38).

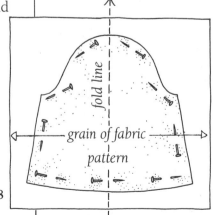

fold line

grain of fabric

pattern

**Fig. 38**

**58** Cut out the pattern pieces and remove the pins and pattern. Fold each sleeve piece wrong side out. Leaving 3/16-inch seam allowance, pin and stitch the seam (Fig. 39).

**Fig. 39**

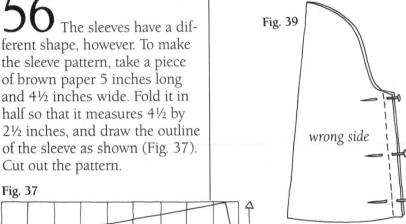

wrong side

**59** Lay both sleeves flat, and clip a 1-inch opening directly on the fold opposite the seam (Fig. 40).

clip 1″

**Fig. 40**

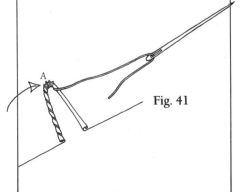

clip 1″

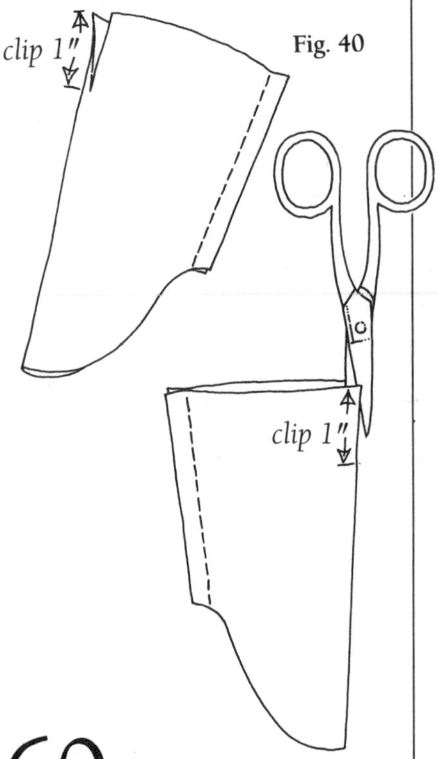

**60** Roll the edges along the cut, and stitch. Reinforce point A with several stitches (Fig. 41).

A

**Fig. 41**

**61** Starting at point B, measure in about ¼ inch and gather the sleeve to C, using a running stitch (Fig. 42). Place the sleeve on the arm of the doll and gather to fit the doll's wrist. Anchor the thread.

**Fig. 42**

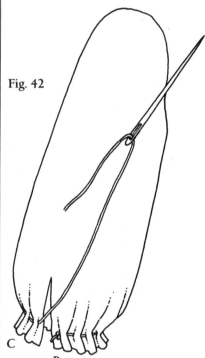

**62** Measure the doll's wrist circumference and cut 2 strips 1 inch longer than the circumference and 1¼ inches wide for the cuffs. Fold in ¼ inch at each end (Fig. 43).

**Fig. 43**

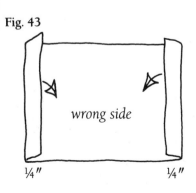

*wrong side*

¼"                    ¼"

**63** With the sleeve right side out, pin the cuff along the gathers, starting at C (Fig. 44). When the cuff is pinned in place, there will be a ½-inch tab (Fig. 45).

**Fig. 44**

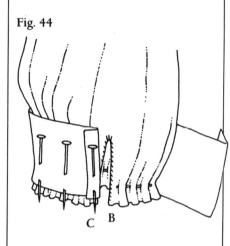

C   B

**Fig. 45**

*right side*

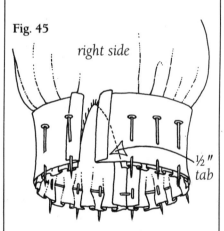

½" tab

**64** Stitch the cuff to the sleeve using a running stitch.

**65** Turn the sleeve inside out, and turn the cuff up. Turn in a narrow hem along the cuff (Fig. 46), then turn over the cuff to meet the gathering line on the sleeve. Pin along the line, then stitch in place.

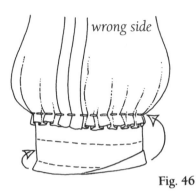

*wrong side*

**Fig. 46**

**66** Stitch the end of the cuff and the end of the tab closed as in Step 54 (Fig. 36).

**67** Sew a small snap in place to close the cuff (Fig. 47), and stitch a small button over the snap on the outside of the cuff to finish it nicely.

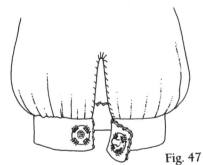

**Fig. 47**

**68** Repeat this process for the other sleeve and cuff. Set in the sleeves, following Step 68 for the clay doll.

# Sewing the Pinafore

**69** To make the pinafore, you will first need to make a paper pattern for the bib pieces. The pattern measurements fit my doll, but since yours might vary slightly in size, compare the measurements given and adjust proportionately if necessary (Fig. 48):

Bib front, 3¼ x 1½ inches
Bib back (left and right
    pieces), 1¾ x 1½ inches
Bib straps, ½ x 2¼ inches

**70** Cut 2 pieces of cotton fabric approximately 12 inches long and 3 inches wide. Pin the 2 layers together, right sides facing. Lay the pattern pieces on the fabric. Pin them in place, mark a ¼-inch seam allowance around each piece, then cut them out.

**71** Remove the pattern pieces and re-pin the fabric layers back together. Stitch the side seams of the bib front closed. Stitch the top seam, leaving a 1-inch opening at each end for inserting the straps (Fig. 49A). Stitch the side seams of each back piece closed. Stitch the top seams closed, leaving 1 corner of each back piece open for inserting the straps (Fig. 49B). Fold the strap pieces in half, and stitch closed (Fig. 49C).

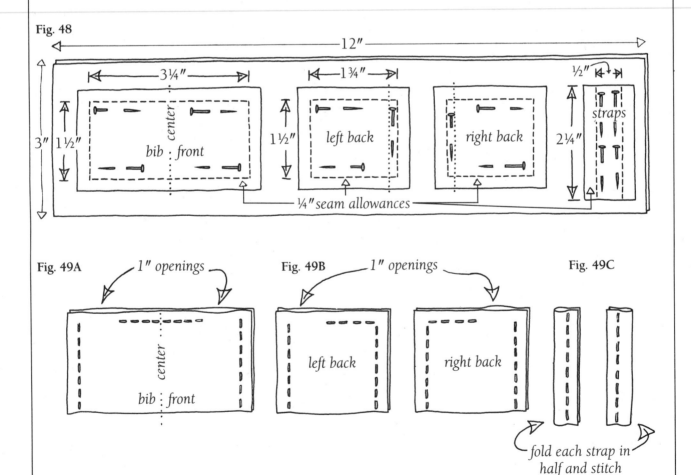

Fig. 48

12″

3″   1½″   3¼″   bib front   center

1½″   1¾″   left back

right back

½″   straps   2¼″

¼″ seam allowances

Fig. 49A   1″ openings

center   bib front

Fig. 49B   1″ openings

left back   right back

Fig. 49C

fold each strap in half and stitch

# 72

Press the seams open and turn all the pieces right side out. Press again. Pin the front bib piece to the front of the dressed doll, and the 2 back pieces to the back, overlapping them at the center back. Pin the shoulder straps in place, tucking them down into the corner openings. Adjust for fit; pin, and stitch closed using an overcast or slipstitch. Sew on snaps to close the back of the bib (Fig. 50). Do not stitch the side seams of the bib.

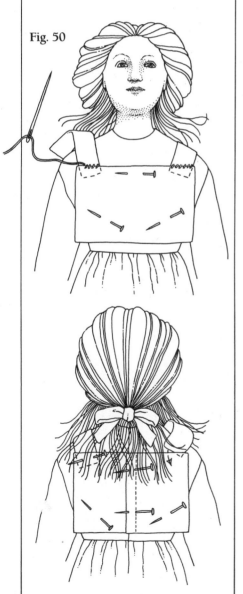

**Fig. 50**

# 73

To make the pinafore skirt, cut out a piece of cotton fabric; for my doll, it's about 28 inches long and 8 inches wide. Make a narrow hem along each end, and make a row of gathering stitches along the top edge. Place the skirt around the doll's waist, and pull the gathering in tightly to fit. Anchor the thread and pin the gathers to the bib.

# 74

Remove the pinafore from the doll. Adjust the skirt and reinforce it with pins as necessary, and stitch around the waist twice to flatten the gathers (Fig. 51).

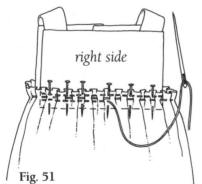

*right side*

**Fig. 51**

# 75

To make the sash, cut out 2 strips of cotton about 20 inches long and 1 inch wide. Press in a ¼-inch seam allowance along both edges of the length (Fig. 52).

*press in*

# 76

Pin the center of one cotton strip to the center front of the pinafore bodice. Pin the bottom edge of the strip around the pinafore skirt. Stitch the sash to the front and back of the bodice and skirt using an overcast stitch (Fig. 53).

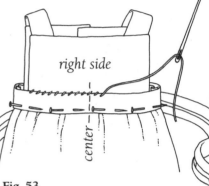

*right side*

*center*

**Fig. 53**

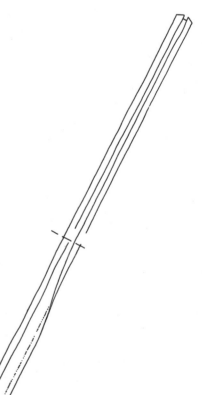

**Fig. 52**

# 77
Turn the pinafore inside out. Pin the second strip to the first, matching the waistband on the outside. Sew to the bodice and skirt using an overcast stitch. Then sew the long sash pieces together using the same stitch. Turn in the sash ends and stitch closed (Fig. 54).

# 78
Hem the pinafore skirt approximately 1½ inches higher than the doll's dress. Slipstitch a strip of lace along the top of the bodice and at the hem of the pinafore (Fig. 55).

**Fig. 55**

**Fig. 54**

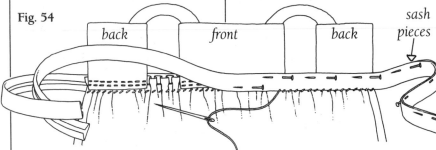

back   front   back   *sash pieces*

# Making the Bloomers

# 79
To make the bloomers, first make a paper pattern. Using Fig. 56 as a guide, trace the outline of the pattern onto paper and add a ¼-inch seam allowance all around. Cut out the pattern.

# 81
Cut out 2 pieces of white cotton fabric approximately 12 inches long and 10 inches wide. Lay them flat and pin them together, matching the grain. Lay your pattern pieces on top, along the grain. Pin them to the fabric, and cut out (Fig. 57).

**Fig. 56**

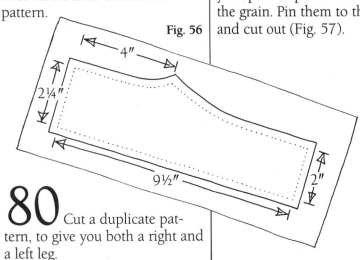

4"

2¼"

9½"

2"

# 80
Cut a duplicate pattern, to give you both a right and a left leg.

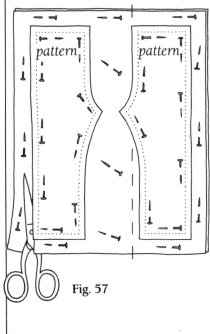

*pattern*   *pattern*

**Fig. 57**

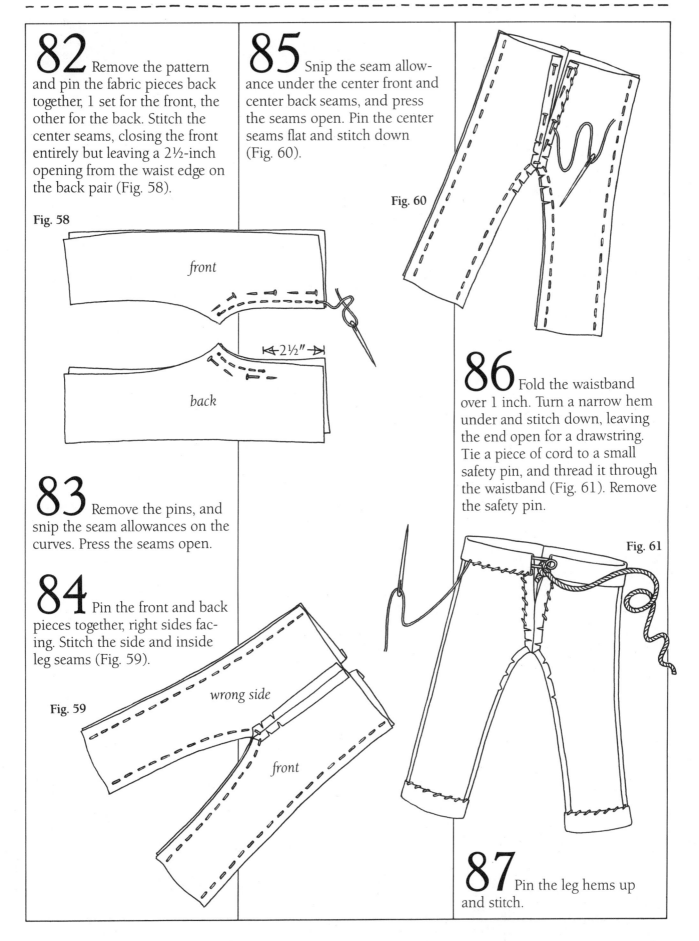

# 82
Remove the pattern and pin the fabric pieces back together, 1 set for the front, the other for the back. Stitch the center seams, closing the front entirely but leaving a 2½-inch opening from the waist edge on the back pair (Fig. 58).

**Fig. 58**

*front*

*back*

←—2½"—→

# 83
Remove the pins, and snip the seam allowances on the curves. Press the seams open.

# 84
Pin the front and back pieces together, right sides facing. Stitch the side and inside leg seams (Fig. 59).

**Fig. 59**

*wrong side*

*front*

# 85
Snip the seam allowance under the center front and center back seams, and press the seams open. Pin the center seams flat and stitch down (Fig. 60).

**Fig. 60**

# 86
Fold the waistband over 1 inch. Turn a narrow hem under and stitch down, leaving the end open for a drawstring. Tie a piece of cord to a small safety pin, and thread it through the waistband (Fig. 61). Remove the safety pin.

**Fig. 61**

# 87
Pin the leg hems up and stitch.

# Making the Stockings

×××××××××××××××××××××××××××××××××××××××××××××××

**88** The fabric for the stockings should be stretchy. If you are making the doll shown here, cut out a piece of this fabric approximately 6 inches long and 4 inches wide and fit it around the leg. Start at the top of the leg and pin the stocking fabric together down the center back to the heel, and under the foot (Fig. 62).

**89** Snip the seam allowance to about ⅜ inch. Turn the edges under, and re-pin the seam into position for stitching. Stitch the seam with an overcast stitch (Fig. 63).

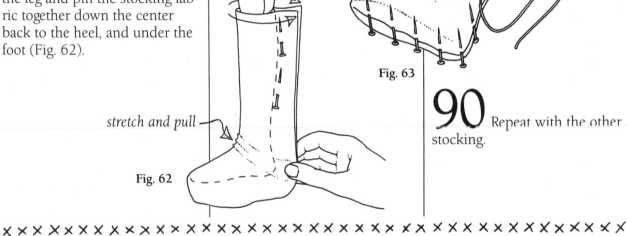

*stretch and pull*

**Fig. 62**

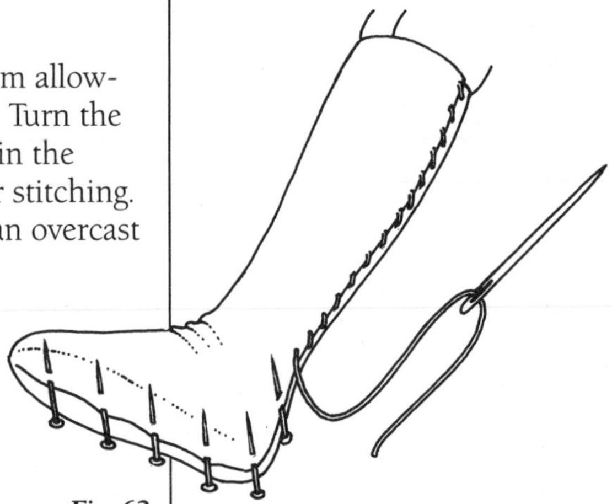

**Fig. 63**

**90** Repeat with the other stocking.

×××××××××××××××××××××××××××××××××××××××××××××××

# Designing the Shoes

×××××××××××××××××××××××××××××××××××××××××××××××

**91** Choose a lightweight fabric for the shoes (heavier cloth is difficult to work with). To make the foot pattern, place the doll's feet on a piece of paper, and trace the outline of each foot. Mark the tracings "left" and "right" and cut them out (Fig. 64).

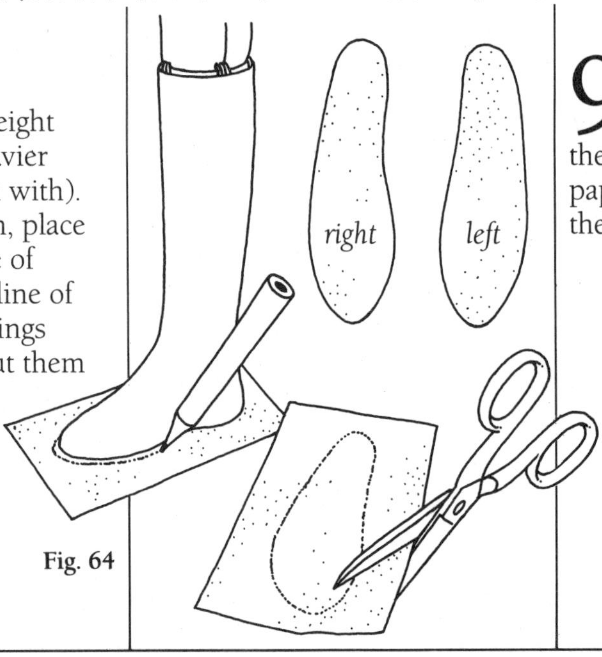

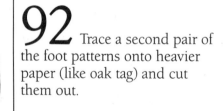

*right*     *left*

**92** Trace a second pair of the foot patterns onto heavier paper (like oak tag) and cut them out.

**Fig. 64**

# 93

Place the heavier pattern pieces on the shoe fabric, and set the thinner paper patterns aside. Trace the patterns onto the fabric with a pencil, adding a ¼-inch seam allowance all around. Cut them out, but do not remove the paper patterns (Fig. 65). Snip the seam allowances (Fig. 66).

**Fig. 65**

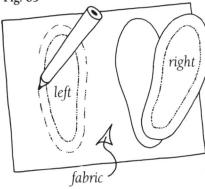

**Fig. 66**

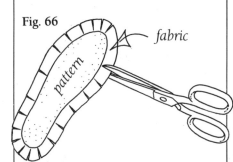

# 94

Lay both foot pieces on a flat surface and coat the edges of the paper patterns with glue. Fold the snipped seam allowance over the paper and press the fabric down (Fig. 67). Set the pieces aside while the glue dries.

**Fig. 67**

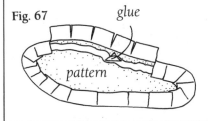

# 95

Cut out 2 strips of shoe fabric 2 inches wide and double the length of the doll's foot. Fold the strips in half lengthways, and press (Fig. 68).

**Fig. 68**

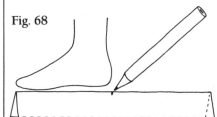

# 96

Mark the center point along the length of the fold, and attach that point to the center of the doll's heel using masking tape. Tape the fabric to each side of the foot, and cut away the excess about ½ inch back from the toes (Fig. 69).

**Fig. 69**

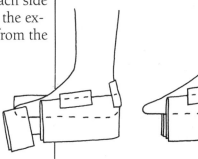

# 97

Cut two 3-inch circles from the same fabric. Fold each 1 in half, and press. Lay the folded circle over the end of the doll's foot, and pin it to the side strip (Fig. 70).

**Fig. 70**

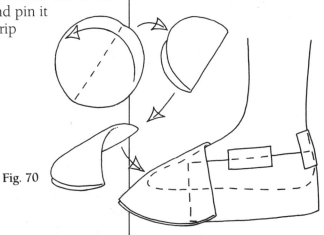

# 98

Cut the excess fabric from around the bottom of the foot, leaving a ⅜-inch overhang. Snip the overhang about every ½ inch (Fig. 71).

**Fig. 71**

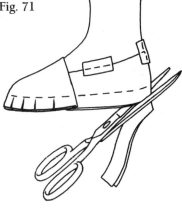

# 99
Put a coat of glue along the edges of the wrong side of the footprint pieces (Fig. 72). Place each footprint piece against the bottom of the doll's foot, with the *fabric-covered* side next to the sole of the foot and the wrong side facing out. Fold the overhang of the shoe over the glue and press down.

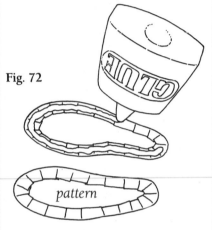

**Fig. 72**

pattern

# 100
Using the reserved paper patterns, trace left and right footprints onto dark brown leather or felt. Cut them out and glue one to the bottom of each shoe (Fig. 73).

**Fig. 73**

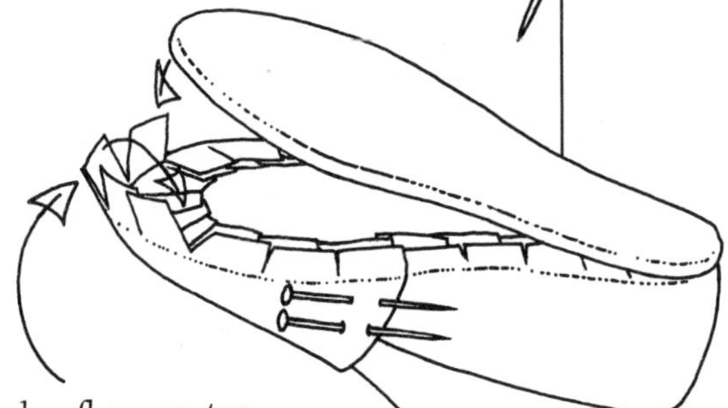

*glue flaps on top of flaps around sole*

# 101
Remove the pins and tape from the sides of the shoes, and stitch the seams (Fig. 74).

**Fig. 74**

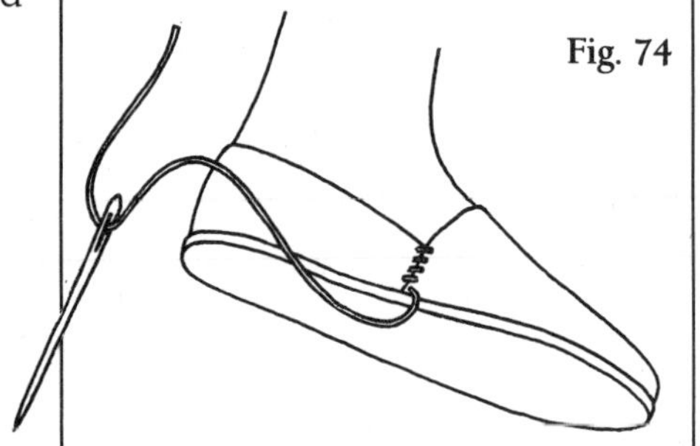

# Making the Hat

# 102
Find an old straw hat with a fine weave, and cut a 6-inch circle from the crown (Fig. 75).

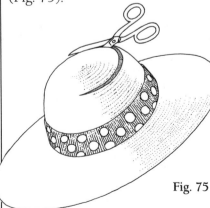

**Fig. 75**

# 103
Press in a ¼-inch hem around the edge (Fig. 76A). When the hem is pressed flat, fold it over another ¼ inch, and press again (Fig. 76B).

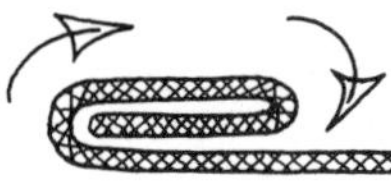

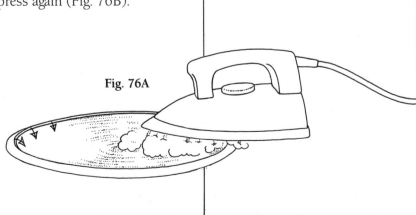

**Fig. 76B**

**Fig. 76A**

# 104

Cut a piece of elastic string long enough to reach from ear to ear under your doll's chin. Tie a small white button to one end and thread the other end onto a darning needle (Fig. 77).

**Fig. 77**

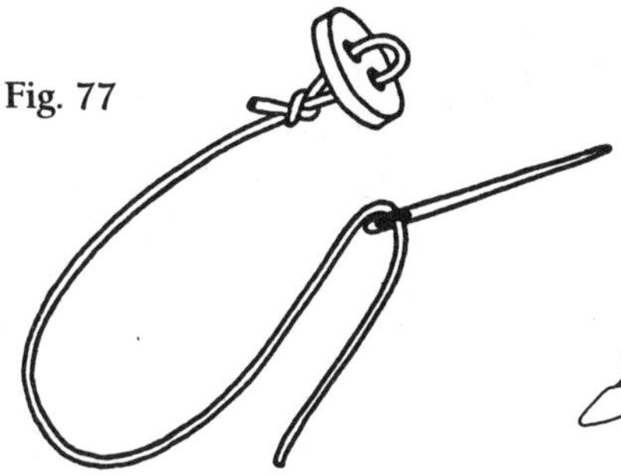

# 105

Mark 2 spots approximately 2 inches in from the edge on each side (Fig. 78). Push the needle through the top of the hat at one of the spots, and pull the thread through until the button lies flat (Fig. 79).

**Fig. 78**

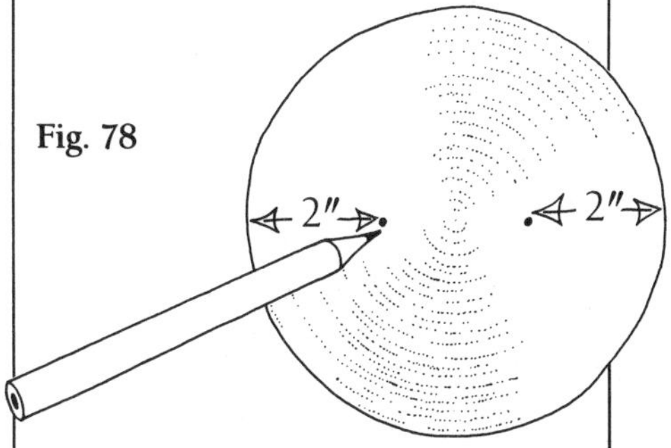

← 2″ →    ← 2″ →

**Fig. 79**

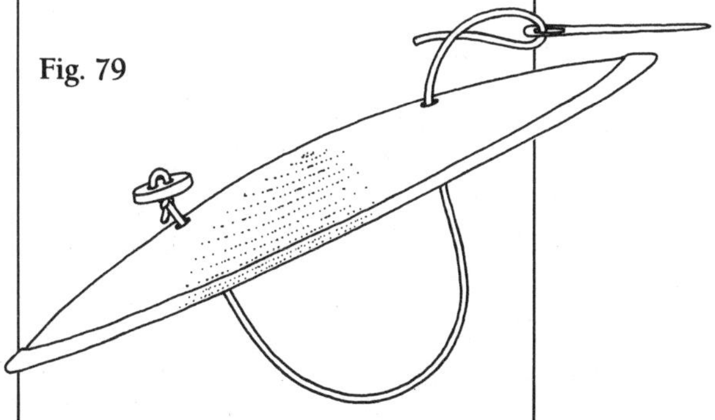

# 106

Bring the needle up through the second spot. Remove the needle, and tie the second button to the end of the elastic. Pull the thread down so that the button lies flat (Fig. 80).

**Fig. 80**

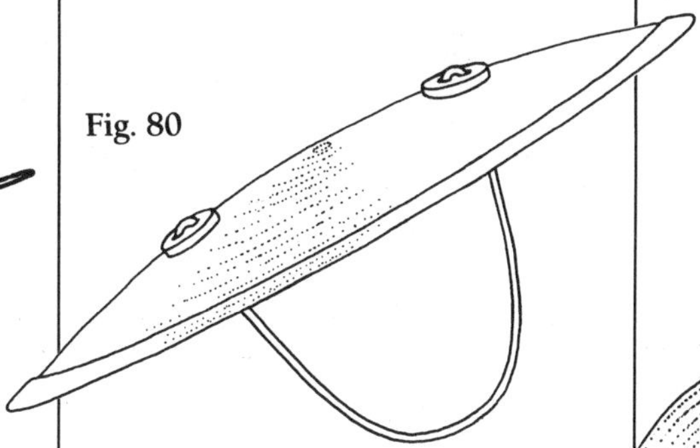

# 107

Congratulations. Now you have your very own wax doll.

# Craft Suppliers

Most materials called for in DOLLMAKING are readily available in local craft and hobby stores, and even five-and-tens. The Yellow Pages is the best way to track down the ones closest to you.

Always keep your eye out for old and interesting fabrics. Some of my best finds have come from Good Will, Salvation Army, and other thrift stores.

If you wish to use mohair for the hair on your clay or wax doll, and have trouble finding it, write or call Dollspart Supplies Company, 5-15 49th Avenue, Long Island City, NY 11101; telephone: (718) 361-0888. They carry mohair and will mail-order it.

The craft clays I recommend for the clay doll are Sculpey and Super Sculpey. They are made by Polyform Products Co., 9420 W. Byron Street, Chicago, IL 60176; telephone: (312) 678-4836. Below is a list of stores in major cities that distribute the clays. Polyform does provide a courtesy mail-order service for retail customers who are unable to obtain their products locally.

**Leisurecrafts Inc.**
3061 Maria Street
Compton, CA 90224
(213) 537-5150

**Pearl Paint Co.**
1033 E. Oakland Park
    Boulevard
Ft. Lauderdale, FL 33334
(305) 564-5700

**Trost Model & Craft**
3129 W. 47th Street
Chicago, IL 60632
(312) 927-1400

**The Brighten-Up Shop**
618 Central Avenue
Great Falls, MT 59401
(406) 453-8273

**S & R Distributing Co.**
714 Greenville Boulevard
Greenville, NC 27834
(919) 756-9565

**A Hobby Hut**
2835 Nostrand Avenue
Brooklyn, NY 11229
(718) 338-2554

**Pearl Paint Co.**
308 Canal Street
New York, NY 10013
(212) 431-7932

**Dupey Management Corp.**
P.O. Box 169029
Irving, TX 75063
(214) 929-8595

**Thomas Wholesale**
5641D General Washington
    Drive
Alexandria, VA 22312
(703) 820-9790

**Craf-T Inc.**
P.O. Box 44577
Tacoma, Wa 98444
(206) 537-5353

**Tri-County Distributors**
2785 S. 167th Street
New Berlin, WI 53151
(414) 782-2120